KEY TRUTHS
OF
OCCULT PHILOSOPHY

AN INTRODUCTION TO THE
CODEX OCCULTUS

MARC EDMUND JONES

*All things are related to all other
things in activity, substance and form*

LOS ANGELES
J. F. ROWNY PRESS
MCMXXV

Kessinger Publishing's Rare Reprints
Thousands of Scarce and Hard-to-Find Books!

TO SARA AND THE MAJOR

IN AFFECTIONATE RECOLLECTION OF FULL
HOURS AND OF MANY FORGOTTEN VISTAS
OPENED TO MEMORY IN THE WALK-UP AT
SOUTH ALBANY WHERE WITH "SOUVENIR"
ON THE VICTROLA AND THE LITTLE CHAPS
ABED BEGAN A TRULY HAPPY IF
MOMENTARY REUNION AFTER
THAT TEMPLE TRAGEDY
OF LONG AGO

CONTENTS

CHAPTER   PAGE

I   THE PERSPECTIVE OF LIFE IN TIME . . . 37

II   THE PERSPECTIVE OF LIFE IN SPACE . . . 61

III   THE DOMAINS OF FORM 87

IV   THE DOMAINS OF CONSCIOUSNESS . . . 114

V   THE DIMENSIONS OF BEING 144

VI   THE DIMENSIONS OF EXPRESSION . . . 167

VII   THE SCHEME OF COSMIC EVOLUTION . . 192

VIII   THE SCHEME OF HUMAN MANIFESTATION . 217

SUPPLEMENTARY MATERIAL

Critical Foreword: The Foundation of Occult Philosophy . 7

Appendix A: The Octonary Constitution of Space . . 254

Appendix B: The Octonary Scheme of Worlds and Man . 255

Appendix C: The Seven Great Keys and Sacraments . . 256

Appendix D: The Septenary Differentiation of Process . 257

Index 258

The pyramid has been broken open;
The square has been laid bare;
The triangle points upward;
The circle will now begin to operate!

KEY TRUTHS OF OCCULT PHILOSOPHY

CRITICAL FOREWORD

THE FOUNDATION OF OCCULT PHILOSOPHY

AN EXAMINATION OF PREMISES

The investigator who seeks to develop exact and careful conception of realities in a realm as temperamental as the occult[1] faces from the beginning unsuspected difficulties. Every defining term as well as every accepted teaching and doctrine is variously interpreted by the different groups of students. Here is a field in which the most sincere teachers are swept into narrow prejudice by the sheer fire of their enthusiasm and so seem universally to emphasize their differences one from the other when they could as well build upon a meeting ground of common understanding.

---

[1]Occultism, occult science and occult philosophy in modern usage loosely refer to all forms of mysticism or magic and to all esoteric or theosophic philosophy and research. With metaphysics which is used in an equally broad but less particular sense they are the general terms for the field. Theosophy is seldom employed except when capitalized in reference to a particular group of societies.

This lack of generally accepted authority demands in critical analysis a preliminary examination and outline of premises. What is occult philosophy? Is it a science?

Philosophy itself is not faith nor dogma but rather search and aspiration for wisdom and knowledge. Science rests upon the accumulation and verification of facts and this is a process which induces wisdom and creates knowledge. Philosophy may properly be considered a department of science. Yet the term occult science sometimes applied to modern metaphysics is hardly proper in the present state of superphysical teaching under claim of authority and revelation especially when belief in the revelation as well as acceptance of the authority must be yielded by the investigator without that intellectual reservation which marks the scientist.

Is occult philosophy a religion?

Religion is the belief of humanity. It may grow upon and be sustained by both science and philosophy although demonstrated knowledge and intuitional wisdom are natural opposites. But philosophy whether occult or otherwise is neither religion nor science. Rather it is the background of each. Aspiration is as necessary to intuition and faith as to scientific investigation. The spiritual zealot is no more constant to an ideal than some less excited worker in a research laboratory.

Any philosophy is built upon consciously developed conceptions of the human mind. Occultism is man's clutch at a superior universe containing both sensual and superorganic beings. All philosophy contributes to science and to religion. Science and religion together add breadth and depth to philosophy. In the never-flickering light of truth little distinction is found between the usefulness of the different members of this intimately associated trio.

The key truths could be based upon the observed and proved evidence of occultism as conveniently as upon the philosophy or common traditions and theories of its students. The objection to such a method here is its tediousness. The facts in comparison with the beliefs are few and are enmeshed in the interpretations of a host of writers who have essayed this method in vindication of their teachings. Furthermore a judicial weighing of evidence against evidence in the realm of objective reality demands of the reader a specially trained mind while a controversial book is of no great use in general circulation.

Of striking interest is the phenomenon of a constant multiplication of occult schools[1] with lengthy lists of supporting students behind each organiza-

---

[1]Few organized occult movements reveal any appreciable development of definite instruction methods. School throughout this treatise rather refers to the body of disciples who follow a teacher or system and to those collectively who hold a philosophical scheme in common or who are actuated by the same spirit, principles and methods. It also occasionally indicates the system, methods and opinions characteristic of those thus associated but herein never identifies an organization visible or invisible.

tion and with established and financially profitable literature to represent each group. Here is found an interested *clientele* which in all-inclusiveness must be numbered in America alone at several millions. This is more than evanescent fascination.

The many leading occultists prominent in other and far more respected fields refute as a group the easy suspicion of charlatanry and of general victimization of the nation's population of credulous ones. While the appeal to the neurasthenic and erotic individual is irresistible and while this subnormal element is to be found in force upon the outer fringe of modern occultism nevertheless the strong and permanent survival of the whole movement gives the surface foolishness no more than momentary interest.

Attention rather must be directed to the deeper appeal of the occult and to the expressions and teachings of the more balanced and earnest pioneers. This must be done not in partisan consideration of differences but in reconstruction and careful gathering of the general acceptance of belief which in later and more detailed scientific analysis may be proved or overturned by conventional methods.

Truth never fears investigation. Verity comes unscathed through any test. Only the bad breath of bigotry insists upon a buttonholed and asphyxiated audience. Only bilious intellectualism fears the purge of true scholarly investigation.

THE EXTENT OF CONFUSION

The primary obstacle to any orderly consideration of occult philosophy lies in the unutterable confusion that disgraces the field. The investigator is
required to labor clear of sharp prejudice and bitter feeling which exist between nearly all established
schools. He must learn and be prepared to identify
in minute detail the bias which seems the hall-mark
of every organized teaching of occultism. He must
perfect a method of allowance for pedantry in his
analysis of principles laid down by members as well
as in his review of literature published by any particular group. Similarly he must discount in rigid
fairness all references and quotations in mutual es-
timates of one another by rival schools.

In pursuance of his purpose the investigator must
establish a foundation which will invite acceptance
throughout the fields of occultism and of competent
general scholarship. He must do more than analyze
the confusion and dismiss lightly the pretenses of
the followers of this and that cult. The lucid truth
of natural law which remains embryonic in this modern sticky mess must be interpreted to the most prej-
udiced intelligence before any broad bias may be
overcome. Science does not labor sufficiently when
it strives only for the conviction of its inner circle
of dispassionate minds. That is self-established su-
periority of the sort which debauches[1] present-age

---

[1]Debauchery is hardly too harsh a word. Common standards of
merit in non-occult fields frequently are abandoned as a mark of

occultism. The justification of any effort is utility. Art and even beauty are esthetically useful in life and are truly necessary to human growth. The initial conquest of confusion in occult philosophy is the building of a foundation upon which practical conceptions and metaphysical sublimities alike may rest.

But antecedent to analysis of fundamental beliefs must come a sympathetic understanding of the extent and causes of the existing confusion.

The text-books are wholly inadequate for any purpose here indicated. A disturbing literary incompetency and a lack of mastery of English as their medium of first expression have marked the three outstanding pioneers self-identified with occult thought and named in following pages among the eight prophets of this new scheme of world philosophy. Two have been edited with some skill but the followers of the first of these have split into rival camps with the result that a branch of one camp has reprinted and reproduced the original volumes with most of their imperfections. Of the other five arbitrarily selected prophets three were Titans of in-

transcendence into metaphysical realms. Thus at least two organizations which particularly teach the necessity for absolute accuracy in all minor details of astrology refuse as groups to attempt the correction of a consistent mispronunciation of seven out of the twenty-nine most frequently used terms in horoscopy. (Aquarius, Aries, Pisces, Sagittarius, sextile, Taurus and Uranus.) Five of these are signs of the zodiac and two other signs out of the twelve (Gemini and Libra) are given wrong pronunciations with noticeable frequency. (Note that in this treatise no identity is given to critical or comparative personalities.)

tellect who would in no wise be complimented by any identification with modern occultism, a fourth was an indefatigable Swiss medical quack while the gentle and obviously impracticable teachings of Christ dramatized in the work of the fifth have come to us several-handed from the Greek original. These last five contribute indeed truly to this newly rediscovered philosophy but not as it is and only as it should be. They are of no assistance in any preliminary labor upon a foundation which so far has been laid by inspired rather than orderly souls.[1]

A characteristic form of snobbery in modern occultism contributes heavily to its disrepute. This is the belief in supersensual revelation for all higher natural law and is the cry of heresy which is raised against anyone who dares to dispute the doctrine.

The value of inspiration and illumination is not underrated in any sensible investigation. The scientist or dispassionate philosopher only insists that the conceptions formulated in the crucible of divine flame be submitted to useful standards when they have been cast and set forth to take their place in a cool and calm world. Instruction is of value not because it comes from a great teacher but because it is available for useful demonstration by every earnest student. A revealer of divine truths is known in the perspective of long years not by the pretensions of his works and the claims of his fol-

[1]For the eight prophets in the order of reference above cf. pp. 166, 60, 141, 190, 215, 252, 113, 86.

lowers but by his pupils in increasing contribution to the progress of his race.

Second in puerility only to the common conception among occult students of a revealed and yet often withheld or esoteric knowledge[1] is the widespread belief in advanced souls or egos.

This theory presupposes that inner teachings of great sacredness are never given except to certain privileged ones. Here as in most departments of thought exists an understratum of truth to account for the doctrine and therefore an analysis of that truth must follow later.[2] The unreasoned assumption which contributes to vast confusion in occult fields is that possession of wide so-called esoteric knowledge is *prima facie* evidence of a highly developed personage. This has led to a broad self-established aristocracy of the world's supposedly spiritually great. Among these well-meaning seekers is a species of log-rolling far more subtle and dangerous than the political chicanery of government or the humorous mutual puffing of artists and literary people.

Here is a cancer which eats deep into the faith of a whole people. To the degree that a student affirms loudly and publicly the spirituality and exclusive knowledge of his accepted occult teacher to that extent does he seem to take on in the eyes of his fellow seekers a measure of the merit and worth

[1]Cf. foot-note p. 56 and esotericism p. 57.
[2]Cf. cycles p. 37, occult tradition and foot-note p. 38, initiation pp. 33, 248 and illumination p. 35.

of the unsuspecting philosopher. And that gentleman by the process is raised to a high unstable pedestal.[1]

If out of the vast membership of the occultly inclined came a host who leavened the world and who participated overwhelmingly in the hard labor of a civilization's salvation some excuse might exist for the log-rolling. But the shallowest thinker once reasoning clearly must understand that any great soul-power requires at least an appreciable outlet in human life and activity. The mark of an advanced soul if men are to be so graded must be in the impress left upon a generation and community. Normal adults are not satisfied with the toys of children nor are possessors of any cosmic consciousness content with the aimless parrot-like rehearsals in secret of mystic histories, sacred keys, revealed numerical and zodiacal schemes, development exercises, lists of heavenly orders of angels and planes and globes or any of esotericism's paraphernalia.

World progress may indeed be said to result eventually from dissatisfactions first nursed in all ages by disgruntled world citizens. Even the confusion of modern occultism serves its purpose if it has created a demand for some scholarly foundation upon which the wide philosophy may rest. The growing public

[1]A great occult organization which was launched with high promise half a century ago has now split into hopelessly antagonistic sections through clashing personalities and this has been coincident in the general student membership with the deliberate deification of the two Hindu occult scholars or *mahatmas* responsible for the movement's inception. Cf. master, adept or initiate, p. 23.

interest might indicate a bubbling of the leaven of truth.   Once baked this new loaf of philosophy might well provide a bread of life.

Through occult nomenclature the extent of confusion in the field first becomes evident to the superficial observer.   No organized system exists at all.   Chaos reigns thoroughly.   Here is the heritage of literary inadequacy bequeathed by the pioneers of the movement as well as the price paid by a present generation for the petty jealousy and aloofness of later and better-schooled followers of the various teachings.

The particular name given to any process, phenomenon or condition in occult philosophy is unimportant.   General acceptance rather than scientific adaptation of root meanings interests the lexicographer. Oral or written expression primarily exists for the interchange of thought and in superphysical realms the language of idea or symbolism rather than words must be employed.   Nevertheless schools of occultism persistently tamper with terminologies as though thereby to maintain their self-asserted claims of intellectual and spiritual supremacy.[1]

[1]The word astral probably possesses greater currency than any other single term in the special field self-identified as occult yet to tell what is meant is impossible without consideration of the affiliation by organization of the writer employing it. Substitution of the word desire in several Rosicrucian groups has not helped the matter but has added to the confusion. Cf. Appendix B, p. 255. For many hampering items of confusion cf. foot-notes pp. 7, 35[2], 59[2], 69, 85[1], 91, 101, 106[1], 127[1], 128[1], 132[3], 140[1], 150[2], 155[1], 155[2], 197[1], 204[2], 205[1], 205[2], 208[2], 208[3], 211[1], 212[2], 234, 235[3].

To an average student of spiritual philosophy the scientific attitude of mind is curiously mysterious. Self-hypnosis through reiteration of this and that form of words gives any seeker a hazy sense of understanding yet such pseudowisdom is far from the incisive analysis which builds a truly pliable and useful knowledge.

All wisdom has its foundation in sensual[1] experience. Evidence gained through the senses results from willing investigation and experiment. The terms or ideas by which a conception is crystallized into conviction are themselves first made real in the being of the investigator before he can proceed. The hypotheses of greater and enlarged experience when extended into superphysical realms must first be taken tentatively. Later they may be subjected to the slow process of test by contributing facts or by conditions that can be proved to the sensual consciousness.

Symbolization is the foundation underlying any occult mastery of the laws related to being. No purely abstract knowledge of nature, God or even man can exist. But nature as a mother, a reservoir or a force; God as a father, a fire or a voice and man as a cosmic pattern, an animal or a divinity all approach understanding. Abstract truth only becomes known through a reflex growth of ideation in the mind. This follows development of related con-

[1]Pertaining to the senses as a whole and in general. This word is best of a bad choice among sensory, sensual and sensuous.

trasting and contributing symbols each capable of sensual proof and objective reality.

All conceptions must be accepted as hypotheses. Any truth must be stated to the child in philosophy figuratively and in a symbol. A willingness to receive any statement without demand for inner or outer conviction and with neither credulity nor skepticism is the happy middle ground of an unbiased and efficiently scientific mind.

Another result of the general chaos in occultism is revealed in the unashamed worship of superphysical phenomena which often completely obscures the real nature and purpose of the philosophy.

The consistent uselessness and incoherence of the average message at spiritualistic séances is typical of the pragmatic value of psychic things in a hard universe of facts.[1] Yet this psychism is deified to a degree barely short of the fundamental personality worship. A claim of supernormal faculties gives the teaching of one claiming them gospel authority to thousands of good citizens even when sober reflection controverts the instruction from every standpoint. Believers will accept any dictation from the unseen

---

[1]References to familiar conditions with reconstruction of identifiable personality and at times with striking foreknowledge of situation are all a fact of spiritualism explained by occult philosophy but these are apart from the checking of ordinary circle messages over a long period which will reveal to any investigator an average usefulness appreciably less than normal human judgment. The true service and valuable place of spiritualism is in its consistent material demonstration of spiritual power.

without question because on some few occasions the unseen has been proved satisfactorily to them and yet will look with commiseration upon trusting souls who purchase without investigation the stock of an oil promoter because someone at another time has made money in petroleum.

No scientist seriously denies supernormal phenomena in fact for all that he may quarrel over terms.

Any good business man is psychic. His judgment obtained by inner flash he calls a hunch or intuition and knows its value. The ear of a musician, the eye of an artist, the taste of a coffee buyer, the fingers of a blind person and the smell of a good cook all present senses developed beyond the capacity of instruments to measure. The materialist recognizes these supersenses without question because of their useful employment in an objective and practical sphere. Any faculty may be developed to its nth degree. Such a process is that expansion of consciousness which in occultism is known as initiation and which is neither miraculous nor mysterious.

Occult philosophy is dragged into disrepute again by the leading-strings of charlatanry. Human nature seeks to substantiate its claims but in this field of abnormal activity the usual pretensions are too wild for easy demonstration. Attempts at objective proof are therefore abortive. Occasionally magic phenomena and now and then startling visitations of the unseen and the not-understood are matters of record. Yet these are hardly the intrusion of outposts from that imagined spiritual realm which is as fantastic in current descriptions as the orthodox heaven. Little is gained by denying phenomena but less is achieved by offhand acceptance of every carelessly projected and unestablished theory.

The line between clairvoyance and imagination is as fine and hard to draw as that between revelation and pure fabrication within. The wish always is parent to the belief. Yet man alone with perhaps a few of his highly domesticated animals can lie and development of imagination necessarily precedes knowledge. In metaphysical philosophy the perversion of truth consciously or unconsciously is a step forward if withal an unsteady one. Truth which follows later is the solvent of knowledge while life is the laboratory for its discovery.

THE LOWERING ETHICAL STANDARD

The principal fruitage of confusion in the field of occult philosophy is the lowering ethical standard of which exaggeration and deliberate misrepresentation are a minor and unimportant phase. The decreasing regard for ideals is a condition dangerous beyond pleasant description.

The physician still cleaves in principle to a Hippocratic oath, the lawyer yields deference to the standards of his fraternity and the priest is true to his vows while the orthodox Protestant minister is faithful to his conscience. In these classes are individual blackguards but a raising of professional ethics is to be noted in practically every established walk of modern life.

The medical organizations for all their bigotry are waging a constant war upon the quack and are yielding not ungracious acceptance to new methods once these are established upon an ethical basis. Disbarment is the quick punishment for malfeasance in legal circles. The churches are inclined to be brutally severe in disciplining men of their cloth. But little protection exists for the public and no restraint is put upon the pander in the field of spiritual philosophy. A heavy price is paid by the modern world for its growing knowledge of supersensual facts. Even the present laws against mediums, astrologers and fortune-tellers are half-heartedly enforced at best.

The professional occultist is at once physician, counselor or confessor and he dictates with entire freedom in matters of soul or body and in affairs of mind or material being. No ecclesiastical hierarchy of the Middle Ages ever ventured the complete control over its *clientele* that is to be found in schools of this growing field. And common metaphysical practice displays an utter lack of adherence even to the standards and ethics which are publicly accepted and taught.

Phallic instruction of the lowest sort is given under guise of spiritual illumination.[1] Immorality and disregard for the simplest obligations of honor

[1] Such as exercises for deliberate control of menstruation.

may be condoned if but a lip and tongue allegiance is paid a teacher or his organization.   Occult principles are specialized for the achievement of money, honors, detachment from obligation, health without cessation of self-indulgence and for every conceivable selfish purpose.   Initiative is taken away by ill-considered predictions of the future.   Character reading and fortune-telling are practiced commonly by students of but a few months' study.

Murder, robbery and rape are not infrequently incited.[1]   The wrecking of homes is accepted as a matter of course.   Innumerable insanity cases are traceable directly to this toying with spiritual dynamite by those who ethically and intellectually are children blundering blindly without supervision and without restraint.   The constant tampering with the human body and consciousness would be gravely humorous if it were a menace less grim.   The wonder is not that occult philosophy frequently stands in disrepute but that honest and sincere seekers ever tolerate an association which cannot but be a general handicap in other walks of life.   No worthwhile student is flattered by the company he is forced to keep.

Nevertheless a very clearly defined system of ethics is taught in this modern miasma of confusion. Two ancient and legitimate purposes still exist for occult study and for interest in superorganic philoso-

---

[1]Cases of each were printed by Los Angeles newspapers in 1924.

phy. These are fundamental and they underlie any superficial reason for investigation.

One is that the seeker may understand himself better in body, mind and consciousness. This is the sole meaning of initiation and is all that is involved in its long and elaborate process. The other purpose is that the student may understand the world more thoroughly in its nature, constitution and evolution. Here absurdly simple and yet extended and wearisome in the taking is the special training which produces the master, adept and initiate much magnified and exalted in the pretense of the occult world.

Understanding of self and service to the world are purposes direct and simple enough to tangle none but the muddle-headed. But until the confusion here outlined in its vast extent is overcome all that is real and basic in occult thought must remain a sealed book to those who possess no Moses in their wilderness.

CHRISTIANITY AND OCCULT PHILOSOPHY

America and Europe in the twentieth century are Christian lands in a Christian era. This though occasionally disputed or ridiculed is a fact that needs little demonstration.

The qualifying adjective Christian as any other word in English means exactly what long usage dictates. The privilege of defining Christianity as a general world religion or philosophy is not the inborn right of any sect or church. The molded attitude of the age and the mass action of the Christian peoples provide the living definition. An orator may thunder his conceptions of what these things should be and to the extent of his power and influence may leaven the whole and contribute appreciably to the meaning. Christ, Paul, Loyola, Luther, Calvin or Wesley in the one instance and Constantine or Cromwell in another have none of them been authors or sole mentors of this third largest world religion and yet Christianity is built and founded solidly upon the struggles, efforts and teachings of these and many thousand others.

What is Christianity? The prophet of Galilee is revealed not in the petty fulminating controversies nor the cheap street profanity that have given publicity to his name through the age but rather in the quiet works and the influence upon national character achieved behind the battle front. In a cosmic scheme little dismay results from bitter struggle and from hard unregenerate feeling. These are the mark of virility and manhood in a general race stock. The symbol of Christianity lies in the hospitals and charities, in the public schools and welfare movements and in the social responsibility and ethics which are a distinguishing product of the past nineteen centuries of conflict.

Science is no enemy to Christianity. The spade of archeology has verified Scriptural stories while philology and textual criticism have confirmed the King James Bible to an amazing extent. Geology has not upset Christian chronology but has rather cleared away established but unwarranted assumptions. The only true sufferers at the hands of investigation have been those who clung not to the clear truth of the Word but to traditions and interpretations which have suited one or another of the many age-old oligarchies of bias.

Modern occultism is Christian because by sheer virtue of that which it alone seeks it is the established philosophy of ultimate abstract truth.

Christianity has contributed an appreciable ethical culture to the progress of a civilized world in which it is a present climax of spiritual aspiration. Christianity stands today the most virile outgrowth of faith found by man through his experience. It willy-nilly has aided modern science in a tremendous development and enormous tabulation of the wisdom and knowledge of human beings.

Closely related to this science and to this religion stands the co-operating agency of philosophy. Occultism is the only all-embracing movement to be found within philosophical realms. The occult field as a whole is truly disorganized and in chaos. The investigator notwithstanding finds a surprisingly broad general meeting ground of fundamental agreement. As this foundation may be scientific so also may it be Christian.

The flame of truth gleams within all world religions. Such is the teaching of each. He who seeks God shall find Him and here is no qualification as to the direction in which the searcher must go. Every religion has that in it which is a unique expression of divine understanding. Occultism only contributes the broad conception that any faith is complementary to any other and that each one reflects light upon and adds illumination to all.

Christianity is known by the doctrine of vicarious atonement. In no other world creed is found the living link of divine offspring whereby the suppliant may gain for his faith a complete share in the nature of God and with it an instant severance of sensual tie to the wheel of life. Among orthodox churchmen the doctrine perhaps becomes hazy upon attempts at explanation but to the hearts of simple men unhampered by reason the truth is crystal clear while at the other extreme of understanding is the master of occult philosophy able to recognize here and to demonstrate a scientific principle of natural law or the transfer of the focus in consciousness from a smaller to a larger cycle of activity.

In Buddhism is found the distinguishing doctrine of *Nirvana* or merging of consciousness misunderstood in the western world as an eventual annihilation of self. Yet this is no more than symbolization of a common phenomenon of selfhood illustrated by the loss of the child's fretful separateness in the social awareness of the adult.

The followers of Mohammed[1] have contributed

---

[1]The Sufis and similar theosophic cults are naturally an exception. The analysis is of conventional or exoteric religion.

true monotheism or a recognition of one divine source as contrasted with the Hebrew worship of one member of a recognized group of gods or the Christian adoration of a deity in threefold aspect. From Mohammedanism the occult philosopher has gleaned that sense of obedience to facts and to the status of any condition which is the keystone of the modern science that had its birth in Arabia under Islam.

From Judaism comes the cabala or keyed knowledge based upon that interrelationship of all things which is the very foundation of occult philosophy. Through Zoroaster and the Persians has been created the popular duality of good and evil which is responsible for the Christian conception of Satan and is revealed in occult philosophy as the polarity of manifestation. Every principle of truth would seem sooner or later to embody itself in the hearts of mankind thereby to germinate into wisdom. For this purpose apparently is a world religion formed around each to create that principle in faith.

Philosophy first and then science is concerned with a complete understanding of all things. Metaphysical philosophy is Christian because the era in which it has grown and the western peoples among whom it is active are so identified. From occultism will come an enlarging of Christianity through a greater understanding of the modern faith and of its foundation in the teachings of the Nazarene. The seeker taught to know himself and to know the world is better fitted as a Christ disciple whether or not that designation pleases him. The frequent effort to paint orthodoxy black adds no degree of whiteness either to an aspirant's understanding or to occult philosophy and supersensual science.

KEY TRUTHS AND FOUNDATION DOCTRINES

A clear distinction must be made between the key truths of the following chapters and the fundamental doctrines here summarized as an underlying basis of the later structure.

The foundation of occult philosophy may be laid down with considerable expectation of accuracy. The doctrines are not untried hypotheses or fresh conceptions but are drawn from the broadly general meeting ground of common understanding. The points of agreement between various discordant schools of thought may be strange to those bound tight by narrow allegiance but they are easily demonstrated. This is so to the extent that some few up-to-date groups are built upon a new and odd intellectual bias. These insist upon a truth limited to the synthesis of all existing occult schools and deny value to the widely different or unique teachings of each particular cult. Here is extremism at the opposite pole in point of view for to occultism dissimilarities are as significant and valuable as likenesses.

The key truths are perhaps new expressions of principles which to the degree that these are correctly stated are as old as truth itself. They are created for a definite useful purpose and are set forth to serve as at least one basic scientific approach in the construction of a simple unified occult philosophy separate and apart from needless controversial emphasis.

In schools of the supersensual and in any religious cult a particular stress must necessarily be laid upon some one aspect of ultimate truth. This singleness in point of view is essential to study and to investigation. Each of the key truths in fact correlates to the general objective of some outstanding division of occult thought and in any analysis of that group and its text-books can serve much as the warp-thread through the weave of a fabric.

The purpose of the whole eight truths as the name implies is to supply an interdependent series of keys to the principles of the entire field. Here the worker stands at the inception rather than at the end of a task. The key truths supplement but do not supplant the various expositions of occult philosophy.

The foundation doctrines are an outline of a stage of growth. They are the expression of the philosophy as it exists. They are determined solely by the fact that they are. Here is the only rock upon which a structure may be built.

Acceptance in belief is not necessary to the investigator but a sympathetic willingness for conviction and a tentative sense of possible truth are quite essential. The occult is a philosophy of life and being too complete and all-inclusive to be put into any simple form of words intelligible to the stranger in the realm. The seeker must swim far into the ocean of metaphysics or else remain discontent and unillumined with the flotsam tossed here and there in the froth of waves at the shore.

What is the sweep or the boundary of occultism in terms of conventional identification?

Occult philosophy is speculation upon natural laws and processes which are yet beyond and above the generally proved and established facts of nature. Loosely all mysticism, magic and theosophical speculation come under this heading. Actually no inclusion must be made of that which has entered so far into the life of civilization as to be no longer philosophical or speculative. An instance is the ritual of the orthodox churches. With sacraments and beliefs in Bible miracles the investigator is not at first concerned for all their significance to occult philosophy. Of importance however are the modern established or recognizable movements which represent humanity's reaching out in advance of its understanding.

Spiritualism must be included with its churches and national conventions and its amateur circles and professional mediums. To these must be added the scientific psychic research groups, modern psychoanalysis and every phase of hypnotism whether on the stage or in medicine. The mystic and philosophical Christian cults are contributing agencies from the one extreme of occult Bible interpretation such as the Russell and Scofield schools to the other of emotional production of phenomena represented by the professional healers and evangelists laboring individually and by the miracle-working groups instanced in the Holy Rollers. By comparison with orthodoxy Swedenborgianism and Mormonism are philosophical and must be included. Transcendentalism, Christian Science, Divine Science, Unity, the Homes of Truth, New Thought and the whole loosely established and unorganized field of Metaphysics[1] with centers and libraries scattered all over the land form perhaps the numerically largest if least cohesive group. The Buddhic teaching is represented by Theosophy with five strong major organizations including the Liberal Catholic Church and by the long list of cults based upon more general Oriental instruction as Bahaism, Mazdaznan,[2] *Vedanta* and many relatively local *yoga* or Eastern science movements. The Masonic, Hermetic or Rosicrucian strain is indicated through orders founded or now headed by Elbert Benjamine, R. Swinburne Clymer, F. Homer Curtiss, Max Heindel, C. Stansfeld-Jones, H. Spencer Lewis, George Winslow Plummer, Rudolf Steiner and some few others. Closely akin to this group is the general pseudoscience classification or the professional and amateur astrologers with quite a few societies or

[1]The self-applied designation of this general group.
[2]Self-coined term for a movement based on Mazdaism.

colleges and an academy, the numerologists[1] unorganized but legion, the palmists who are generally professional and also spiritualists, the phrenologists and other character-analysts or vocational counselors and the many medical cults which are mostly dietetical but include the occult methods of disease determination like Iridiagnosis[2] and those combined with supersensual treatment represented by the Electronic Reactions of Abrams. Here is the broad general experimental field of occult philosophy in the United States alone.

The foundation doctrines are seven in number. Recognition of these will not be necessarily in the form stated here. Some groups deny particular teachings based upon certain of the principles. But acceptance of these is almost universal in the realm of occultism.[3]

THE FOUNDATION DOCTRINES

The doctrine of the microcosm is first of the foundation seven. In its common form it is the Hermetic axiom "As above, so below." The microcosm or little world is man who combines within himself all the elements of the greater world or the

[1] Numerology as the current word for the occult science of numbers is not recognized by the dictionaries.

[2] A coined word for diagnosis by charting the spots and lines in the iris of the eye.

[3] Largely explained by the overlapping *clientele* of all established occult movements. It is a rare student who will confine himself to one school. A *questionnaire* in a typical lecture audience in 1923 revealed an average of three present or past radically diverse occult affiliations.

macrocosm. Upon this doctrine is based the whole scheme of astrology which measures and deduces from movements of the planets through the zodiac or heavenly man the influences to be expected in some terrestrial counterpart. In conventional Christianity it is the creation of man in the image of God.

Second is the doctrine of initiation or special training of human beings to fit them for spiritual or superphysical responsibilities. Scientifically this is the recognized aphorism that special knowledge requires special faculties produced by special training. A physician who is a specialist in certain disorders may in the meaning of the occult term be called an initiate. In the Bible this doctrine is the command of the Nazarene to the faithful to become themselves Christs and is the clear explanation of that teacher's exegesis of the eighty-second psalm.[1]

Third is the doctrine of transmutation or the continuity and inherent indestructibility of matter which modern science has most thoroughly proved. Indeed some few of the cycles of change from element into element have been demonstrated by savants in fair vindication of alchemy. The orthodox church in its creed is interested in this doctrine more than it suspects for here is the resurrection of the body which is adroitly misexplained by the average doctor of divinity. In history this doctrine lies behind mummification since the ancients knew the responsibility

---

[1] John, 10: 34-36.

of the spirit within to any clay which is once in-habited by it and thus specialized to its use.

The doctrine of *karma* is fourth and is the most familiar of all to the general public. Superficially science seems as little concerned with this doctrine as is conventional religion with the third. But scholars are beginning to suspect that nothing in the sensual world is without importance and with-out meaning. Materialistic man stands ready to believe that when all contributing causes are known neither accident nor coincidence exists in any event of life. To religion this is the old eye for an eye and the sins of the fathers visited upon the children. The occult philosopher quickly learns that the son of the father is the spirit itself cast again in a new experience and there able to settle debts and to balance a development carried over incomplete from former efforts.

Fifth is the doctrine of operative magic or the belief in supernormal phenomena. To the scientist this is intelligible as a statement of universal gravita-tion or a theory established as long ago as Newton. All influence and power in the universe is funda-mentally identical. The more closely cosmic force can be carried back to its undifferentiated aspect the more easily magical results may be achieved. Science will distrust but it will no longer doubt any phenom-enon. Too many wonders have been produced and reproduced in the laboratory. Through religion a belief in miracles has survived from oldest times and now is only denied in that peculiar modern church which stands a masquerading shell of faith. The occultist knows that magic is not suspension of ordinary cosmic law but is operation of higher natural principle and so he quarrels with neither faith nor science.

Sixth is the doctrine of reincarnation or the storm-center teaching among occultists. It is far more rooted in general belief than ever suspected. To the scientist who will have nothing of it the doctrine is important as the continuity of intelligence which is the corollary of the third doctrine. In the East it is universally accepted and that acceptance is represented in America by Theosophy[1]. From that extreme follows a confused gradation of belief in this doctrine down to the stand of the conventional Christian church which believes as did the ancient Jews in reincarnation for great leaders only as in the case of Elijah reborn as John the Baptist.[2]

The doctrine of illumination is last of the series. In its fullest expression it is an affirmation that man

[1]To an amusing degree in one largely sold text-book where the dying person of the future is portrayed in the selection of his new parents who then proceed to marry upon his death and to accommodate him immediately after his funeral.

[2]Transmigration or the theory of a life cycle through animals after human experience while sometimes confused with reincarnation is no part of occult philosophy and never has been. Rather it has grown out of the rare obsession of animal form by earth-bound human spirits and the occasional degeneration of human egos into animal form as extreme retrogression after a long series of lives. (Cf. p. 88.) Metempsychosis is a term which inclusive of both reincarnation and transmigration is seldom used by occultists. Rebirth is a Rosicrucian substitution for reincarnation.

may attain to a complete knowledge of the spiritual while yet incarnate[1] and this is a principle peculiar to metaphysics. It is a necessary companion to the second doctrine in any forward progress of occult philosophy as a whole. Science gives grudging assent to the aphorism that anything which man can imagine he eventually may achieve and the truth illustrated in this doctrine has kept savants driving on at tasks that more often than not have seemed hopeless and empty. Through all religion and in the Christian church especially has been found springing ever-alive in the hearts of men the hope and expectation of a full and satisfactory understanding to come. In occultism this dream of divine wisdom is not postponed to a future indefinite heaven state but is promised and indeed given to the earnest student in the living now and here.

[1]Ritual of the Societas Rosicruciana in America.

CHAPTER I

The Perspective of Life in Time

TIME IS ILLUSION[1]

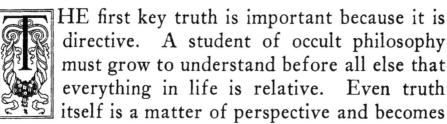THE first key truth is important because it is directive. A student of occult philosophy must grow to understand before all else that everything in life is relative. Even truth itself is a matter of perspective and becomes pseudotruth or perhaps broad error when the point of view is from a bias. Truth itself is too abstract and subjective to be stated in any form of words without some necessity of qualification and indeed two and two make four only as a matter of mathematical addition of comparable ideas or objects.

The purpose of this initial key truth is that the mind of a voyager into the realm of the occult may be freed from an inhibition staggering to any true understanding of superphysical phenomena. Time to the human race is somehow fixed as the perfect symbol of exactness. This sense of accuracy of duration is so ingrained that a grasp of cycles or the cooperation of time measures is supposed in occult

[1]The key truths are given in the first subheading of each chapter.

tradition[1] to be the one inner instruction reserved for the highest of adepts and masters and so forever withheld from open teaching.

But modern science in a splendid intuition born of unselfish never-tiring study and investigation has clutched at truth and caught a fragment in the familiar aphorism that time is dimension. The occultist learns that time has no being of its own but is merely an indicating, qualifying and measuring condition.

Sentient reality cradled in duration is illusion from the perspective of higher realm and deeper being. Time in the objective sphere of length, breadth and thickness is a fourth-dimensional limitation while in that fluidic realm of four dimensions next superior to this the quality of duration becomes a fifth dimension.[2] In the conceptions of occult philosophy ab-

[1]Occult tradition is the teaching taken from the secret records of the great brotherhoods. These records are not archives at inaccessible monasteries although many ancient manuscripts are so preserved. But the life of skin or prepared leaf is short against a perspective of many hundred thousands of years so that all physically preserved writings must be transcribed from time to time. Neither are these taken from the *akasa* or memory of nature. All clairvoyant reading is tinctured necessarily with the personality of the medium and such investigation is worthless unless checked against other sources. The secret records of the brotherhoods rather are that tradition which establishes itself in a uniformity of truth through slender deviation in a mean of facts turning up constantly in the recreated divine philosophy given forth by inspired teachers in regular succession and order. In this manner basic truth automatically adjusts its expression to the evolution both of man and cosmos. These records fundamentally are secret because they only first reveal themselves through higher signatures which are necessarily the possession of initiates.
[2]A fact curiously noticeable in clairvoyance is that the reading of the past and future of a person and thing at hand or a transcend-

stract time is the dimension of separation between any two immediately inferior and superior realms of consciousness. The lesser sphere always becomes illusionary or ephemeral to the greater being.

Time is the expression of the veil between dimensions. Any effort to exalt the consciousness above the limitation of material being demands operative concepts[1] of which the first is based upon the reversal of normal processes in point of view from realm into realm. This requires a new perspective from the little sphere of present life out into the larger domain that embraces all being. Since objective existence is illusion to the enclosing broader reality then in the light of necessary perspective a sense of this present or immediate impermanence of being must be gained as a foundation of greater perception.

Most frequently the seeker strays at this point from the straight path of logic or from the way of mental and scientific attainment. Occult knowledge hardly requires that material reality be denied or that a race plunge itself into ineptitude and decay as that philosophic East which is content with an unsanitary and far from lovely imitation *Nirvana* on earth. The sense of illusion in the consciousness needs but one practical application and that is to

ence of time is simple and common in comparison with the viewing of contemporary events and scenes in that conquest of space which superficially would seem easier.

[1]Because of the inherent superorganic nature of occult teaching it must be built entirely upon these operative concepts or symbols which are not form pictures but are types or patterns of mental process. Cf. p. 17 and foot-notes pp. 53, 70[1].

the qualifying and limiting outer dimension of the more crystallized realm or the factor of time. Philosophically the first key truth becomes the statement that time is illusion.

The consciousness of time illusion is easily gained.

THE UNCERTAIN NATURE OF TIME

Few things as scientifically inexact as the modern duration measures are yet assumed by the layman to be as reliable and perhaps as wholly perfect. From the rather unsuccessful synchronization of the clocks in a city by telegraph to the unsatisfactory calendar all time records are baffling in their inherent confusion. The moon despite Newcomb's labors cannot be forecast with decent accuracy. The sun which is more consistently erratic by comparison is off schedule on all but four days in the year and at times by as much as fifteen minutes. The Gregorian calendar in order to maintain the equinox in its proper place and to rectify the error of the Julian reckoning[1] omits the intercalary day in every even hundred year as eighteen or nineteen hundred but yet reestablishes the leap-year if the even hundred is divisible by four hundred as in the case of sixteen or twenty hundred and even this elaborate procedure is not exactly accurate. So much for mathematical measure!

Time and duration in actual life are never truly

[1] The Julian reckoning is thirteen days behind Gregorian for Julian dates subsequent to February 29, 1900.

synonymous. It may and may not be a quibble to say that an aphasia victim has lived a shorter time than his fellows by the days or months of his aberration or to claim that in years Rip Van Winkle was considerably older than in existence. If the philosopher would demonstrate the correctness of such a contention he must turn to point of view and to definition and must gain an understanding of perspective. Both this and the more conventional understanding can be truth.

No speciousness prevails in the fact that if twins voyage around the world in opposite directions one will be two days older than the other upon their return to a starting place. When they reach the Pacific Ocean and the international date line one goes back a day and lives it over while the other is forced to bridge a day that is never lived. This is true although the one traveling west passes an hour twice at each fifteen degrees of longitude and loses the day at the meridian of adjustment to compensate for the whole twenty-four while the eastward voyager gains the day at the date line to adjust an hour lost for each fifteen degrees traveled. In other words the watches carried by each if maintained in the time of the starting place would at the conclusion of the two trips agree even if they showed days and months as well as minutes and hours. From the perspective of that time measure which indicates hour periods of a mean sun transit brought about by the earth's constant revolution the twins have remained the same age. But the one who travels west has circled the earth with the sun and escaped a transit while in the case of the other the sun actually rises, culminates and sets on two complete days which the former never lives.

The telegraph and wireless demonstrate curious conflicts of time measure while daylight saving ordinances contribute or subtract an extra hour here and there. The photograph and phonograph destroy duration by partial reproduction of scene or voice. The cinema news-reel adds motion to the photograph while the enacted moving-picture may truly conjure up anew and reproduce in visual actuality some forgotten epoch or historical event. These are mechanical and scientific devices more wonderful and miraculous than any simple supersensual development of bodily faculty.

Yet it is in consciousness or the expression of sentient being that the illusionary nature of time may best be demonstrated since through the extension of sense faculty physical duration is transcended and the illusion of eternal substance first conquered.

Deep philosophy lies in the story of the illiterate peasant who in constant complaint of his lot drew the devil to him.

"If you'll agree to give me your soul at the end of a year," said the tempter, "I'll grant you within that time everything you wish provided only you ask for nothing to destroy our bargain."

The peasant agreed with alacrity. He specified great wealth, rare wines, beautiful women and all the exotic things of sense. He did not neglect necessary improvements in his own person, appearance and graces.

Satan as seems to be customary with nether majesty promptly fulfilled his part of the agreement. Then one day he appeared to his victim and tapped him on the shoulder to tell him his time had come.

The transformed peasant was most indignant. He sputtered and explained that only seven months had passed.

The devil smiled. "You have lived your year in seven months!" he answered.

Duration or length of time depends upon consciousness. Even to the physical eye that part of a watched five minutes in which the large hand passes over the hour mark upon the clock dial is considerably longer than a mathematically equal period before or following. Partly optical illusion this yet illustrates a very important law of the *Codex Occultus*[1] and provides a simple demonstration of the illusionary nature of duration to the senses.

The personal interest factor in time has enriched the idiom of all language. A day is long or short not by its season but by what occurs within its duration. An hour drags or a month speeds by. To comprehend deity man says that a year is a day in divine

[1]The law of pattern in the recapitulation group of the phallic key under the tetrad.

sight. A strong impression persists in its yesterday while a hope deferred stretches an eon ahead.

In occult philosophy the very inexactness of duration measures in mathematical relationship and in terms of consciousness becomes the clue to many grades of understanding. All this is based most simply upon the key truth that time is illusion. The significance is not that time has no existence but that cycles or duration measures are the indicators and guides to understanding of all sense perception which from the perspective of an enlarged consciousness is illusion and so relatively impermanent and transitory.

LIFE PERSPECTIVES IN TIME

An understanding of life through the philosophical point of view more readily adapts itself to periods of time than to divisions of space or to analysis of substance.[1] The units of duration are part of almost every conscious human thought. From that eternity of heaven or hell which is the cudgel held by the church over the masses to the never unspoken "What shall we do tonight?" man pigeonholes his philosophies and appetites according to the exigencies of the calendar or the clock. When faced with death his only wish is time. The commonest human phenomenon or sleep but creates a duration unit. The sternest life necessity or food

[1]Space is the consideration of the following chapter and substance of the third and fourth chapters.

establishes a cycle of meals. Denial of a wish or satiation of a desire in strengthening the one or killing the other reveals a simple element of human psychology wholly dependent upon the factor of duration. These essentials apart from all considerations of occult philosophy would establish the initial key truth as the first.

Occult philosophy recognizes eight important time units. Of these the second, minute and hour are too fine in their coordinate supersensual application and too attenuated in ordinary human experience to be of particular interest here other than as mathematical subdivisions of larger measures. But in company with the other five they have occult power and individual characteristics particularly to be noted in astrology. In general the occultist learns that each or any one of all eight of these time units possesses a life and activity distinction of its own.

Christmas or Easter is a day while other twenty-four hour periods are lesser dignities. The Holy Week is a living, throbbing, vital and powerful succession of sacred moments which only can be called a week. So is the month more than a mathematical calendar division. A difference exists in years as between the nineteen-fourteen and nineteen-eighteen of recent experience. The life epoch, eon or eternity provides the always varying boundary of inclusion for a totality of human time cognition in any particular field.

In occult philosophy the basic unit of all time measure is the day because that period of waking hours is the ordinary normal cycle of continuous human consciousness. A day lies between two transits of the sun over the nadir or refers occultly and ordinarily to any fundamental cycle of consciousness in activity. *Der Tag* meant not the opening of war but the expected achievement and so the period of fighting involved. Every man may have his day and thus history speaks of the day of Washington or of Cæsar. In the Bible an era of creation is the same simple unit. In modern practice it is the sum of working hours for which man is paid and is also the work accomplished or the distance traveled in a waking period. A day of Brahma is the whole duration of the present universe from first activity to eventual rest or a *manvantara*.

Every duration unit possesses character.

Time is no less real than substance since all matter in the sense of ultimate reality is illusion. Illusion is a technical word that is in no wise synonymous with delusion. Many who seek to understand the occult hypothesis of life lead themselves astray at the outset because they attempt to see in matter and objective form nothing but a miasma of nightmare. The created world is a thin shadow of invisible power but it remains nevertheless the only reality for one whose higher consciousness lies undeveloped. Only through the familiar crystallized sphere of being can the ego of man mount in understanding.

Time is illusion because duration supports and contains substance. All is illusion because substance and time are actually interchangeable. Frequently in America until its civilization grew out of balance a dollar and a day stood one for the other.

Any unit of time has form as well as character. Although this is abstract it is no less actual than the concrete form of matter.

A day is formed by the routine which gives it individuality. Sleep at its beginning and at its end and between these the succession of meals and little panderings to minor appetites all mark the skeleton. The greatest of sensual experience in a mating of polarities is placed normally at this little cycle's climax. These three first natural desires of man are sought by him to complete this basic duration period of being. In direct proportion to the degree of interest or created illusion in passing events the day is shortened to the consciousness while its form becomes full. Scientifically the day is of fixed length but in philosophy it is an important cross-section of consciousness as actual as material substance and so is as varied as is life itself.

Similarly the week gains form through the difference in days. It contains a Sabbath, sometimes a holiday or more and usually a pay check and at least one night of some sort of dissipation. The month embraces its weeks and calendar events, its financial recurrences and its moving menstrual cycle. The year is made up of months grouped in seasons with

lease periods and income taxes and with summer
vacation and winter clothes. The life is first marked
by experience from infancy through adolescence and
youth. Age is halted or advanced by romance or
study and by journeying in imagination or in actuality.

These are perspectives of life in time.

THE INTERCHANGEABILITY OF TIME MEASURES

In yielding potency to a unit of duration *per se*
the occultist first steps thigh-deep into the depths of
his all-embracing philosophy. Here the progress of
the investigator begins with an understanding of
that fundamental philosophic conception known as
the golden truth of occultism and found in the statement that all things are related to all other things
in activity, substance and form.[1]   No part of creation stands alone in the universe yet everything in its
own sphere is individual and independent.

Only as a matter of faith can the human brain
first realize that no really discordant notes are found
in the harmony of God's creation.[2]   Around man is
all the outrageous injustice and grim hard necessity
of existence. No conscientious citizen of the world
can close his eyes and heart to this in intellectual
denial. Self-centered seekers who dwell in empyrean

---

[1]Cf. title-page and p. 95.   The key truths are no more than expositions of this golden truth.

[2]Occult philosophy is pantheistic in its science but monotheistic in
its faith and it therefore robs neither man nor God of deity. God
is the convenient generic term for any activity or purpose divine to
human consciousness.

nothingness do real injury to occultism and to its
true beauty of concept.

As an untrained auditor attends an opera such as
Tristan und Isolde and hears only discord so man
sees in life nothing but woe until his senses and
mental faculties are directed to the correlation of
causes and effects and to the bridging of less interwoven events by that consciousness of a greater relationship lying behind. The difference between
one great teacher and his disciples was that Christ
alone saw the glistening ivory of beautiful teeth and
in the spell of that glint caught by other senses none
of the stench from a dog's carcass upon the road.[1]
The adept will detect deep through every ordeal of
life the good and divine purpose achieved and so will
know the full harmony of evolution.

The occultist understands that knowledge primarily results from the coordination of relationships.
This fundamentally is the science of astrology which
in the present era is perverted[2] to a delineation of
horoscopes and a prediction of events. Yet through
nativities and astrological fortune-telling is a useful
purpose served because of the drill provided in in-
terchangeability of time units. A day stands for a
year as do four minutes or a month. This and

[1] A narrative preserved in the records of an Eastern mystic order
and found also in the stories of other world teachers.
[2] Perversion is not an unmerited designation in view of the general incompetence of delineations. E.g. in 1915 the president of the
largest society of astrologers in America had three times mistakenly
predicted his own death and upon the first occasion had given away
many of his effects in preparation for the event.

the lesser interchange of irregular cycles may be demonstrated by any careful worker without previous knowledge in a relatively short tussle with any of the more competent astrological text-books.[1]

All nature demonstrates the unity of related time periods when they are taken without consideration of the astronomical divisions which give clock measure. This is through alternation in perspectives of life in time and is first achieved by use of domain or the field of observation in point of view.

Parturition with its contributory phenomena while wholly regular in itself yet varies widely with species and in man with individuals. Biology shows the regularity of type in life cycles where each will pattern the other but with so great a variation in calendar duration as between insects which are born and die in one day and reptilia known to live for centuries. Sleep is associated with recurrence of night but also with a winter slumber of animals that hibernate. Life itself generally is seasonal and develops in cooperation with the year or its subdivisions yet wholly odd visitations of species are known such as the periodical cicada.[2] Botany displays trees like the Eucalyptus which grow with amazing strength and rapidity or the Sequoias which in some species are so slow-growing and so powerfully resistant to the axe of man and to cataclysm

[1]E. g. *The Progressed Horoscope*, Alan Leo (London 1905) and perhaps preceding volumes of this series for necessary preliminary instruction.
[2]Seventeen-year locusts is the familiar term but a misnomer.

that the age of individuals is staggering and of the species beyond calculation. In some countries plants are annuals that are perennials in other lands.

In physiology the systole and diastole cycle is the sustenance of objective existence and is subject to every disturbance without loss of its power to revert to regularity. It is a time unit and a phase of life which has character and form for all that physical science cannot understand nor explain it. Sleeping and waking are common phenomena and are the systole and diastole of a larger cycle which with aphasia or under hypnotism may also show startling but transient irregularity.

These units of duration are therefore only to be understood by change in point of view. The shift in field of perspective or plane of understanding involves domain which is the sphere of particular being. Natural law shows that all activity, substance and form is normal and regular within the domain of a proper focus of consciousness. Apparent irregularity is the result of concurrent activity, substance and form in some other domain and is to be found normal with a sufficient widening of understanding.[1]

The second and other type of alternation in perspectives of life in time is by use of cycle in analysis of phenomena repetition. As all activity, substance or form is normal in its proper domain so must every measurable or cognizable expression of being be normal and orderly in the routine of its con-

[1] Cf. the occult conception of domain, p. 90 ff.

sciousness through this activity, substance and form. In nature is found an interrelationship of duration expression in which smaller cycles are always contained in larger and in which the coordinate processes of recapitulation or combination and attenuation or division permit all change whether in growth or decay. This is a fundamental understanding on which the whole of the ancient mysteries was built and is a conception which was carefully withheld from public teaching until its discovery by scholars as a fact of chemistry.[1]

The primer instruction in cycles is given to occult students through astrology. The earth possesses three motions in its axial rotation, its orbital revolution and the shifting obliquity of the equatorial plane in reference to the ecliptic. The first produces days, the second years and the third epochs of crea-

[1]Principally embodied in the chemical laws discovered as conservation of mass (Lavoisier), multiple proportions (Dalton) and the periodic system (Newlands, Meyer and Mendeleeff). The elements or the basic constituents of substance are indestructible. Balance as the quantitative check in chemical analysis becomes in occultism that factor of domain whereby change in any smaller cycle is permitted by the relative fixity of the larger. Occult analysis of activity is duplicated by the chemist through the second chemical law cited. The same two substances may combine in various proportions but a simple ratio which always exists between the different and progressive possible results reveals here the mathematical basis of all cycles as taught in occult philosophy. The chemical law of structure now evolved into the periodic system was the materialist's new discovery of the basic occult principle underlying form. This investigation of chemistry demonstrated that identity in properties necessitates identity in structure. Obviously the conclusions drawn by material scholars themselves may vary widely from the occultist's interpretation of their work. Cf. foot-note on page following.

tive manifestation.[1] To these duration units nature adapts herself. The directional or predictive astrology of nativities is based upon the interchange of various time divisions due to the corresponding earth motions. The nativity or horoscope itself is built upon the deeper truth in the relationship not of interchangeable units of equality in different domains by which the four minutes of rotation and the day of revolution measure in each case to the year of individual life but in the relationship of some division or duration phase of a larger cycle to the whole of a smaller contributory period.

The human embryo is initially a cell and is then a living structure of increasing complexity that grows through a succession of exact correspondences to all basic forms of sentient life in the order of general evolution so as to climax itself in its human state where at first it is only a general type of the whole race but where it may develop into individuality by

[1]The occult hypothesis of the third motion and the whole theory of succession in epochs and geological changes differ radically from the views of material science as will grow increasingly evident to the reader unfamiliar with superorganic tradition and teaching. Since the hypotheses of metaphysical philosophy serve only as operative concepts the external and contributory demonstration of any one of them would be to no purpose in the present treatise. (Cf. footnote p. 39.) The abstruse paragraph preceding in the text is an important summarizing and foundation concept which gains clarity through its employment yet if it were copiously foot-noted and amplified it would confuse and interrupt the careful building of a larger conception containing it. The demonstration of the dolphin-like dive of consciousness in and out of manifest expression and the particular consideration of recapitulation and attenuation follow at proper points in the text and are of no detailed significance here. For this essential paring of details cf. p. 57.

equally interesting stages of correspondence through the succession of changes in consciousness which mark human evolution. This is recapitulation. Here is a definite set procedure to be found in all growth.

In subordinate functions man incorporates the vegetable and mineral kingdoms within his animal-kingdom form. The growth of abnormality like disease or malignant decay is as regular and normal within its sphere as is any other form of natural activity.[1] From a cross-section of any stage and state of evolutionary process the past may be known and the future predicted accurately. Bones are built into true plaster models of prehistoric beasts never seen by the restorers. The medical expert learns the outcome of a disease from a microscopic bit of germ culture. Diagnosis and all keen judgment are thus founded. Were it not for this cyclic and immutable regularity of natural law man's lot upon the globe would be hopeless while creation would be chaotic.

The occult scientist progresses beyond his associates in the physical realm by his insistence upon the extension of objective law for the understanding of subjective phenomena. The botanist in the seed of the lotus sees the plant to be while the occultist in the vague gropings of the human mind sees the world to come and so recognizes in potential fact the new heaven and earth of inspired prophecy. The

[1] Cf. *rigor mortis*, p. 137.

scholar in metaphysical philosophy well knows that anything which the imagination of man can visualize man himself can achieve.[1]

Recapitulation in activity is recognized by physical science. This recognition has resulted in methods of education and crime detection without the slightest lay realization that the tendency of a certain type of mind or bodily make-up towards a definite course of action and reaction is purest astrology and occultism. Recapitulation in form or reduplication is equally recognized through heredity or eugenics and in breeding of animals and botancial culture. The occultist only progresses beyond this conventional acceptance in taking his thoroughly logical step forward. The intelligent ego or being around and upon which all life and activity center must itself be subject to these same laws of cycle.

Consciousness recapitulates in activity and so human growth is achieved in noticeable waves of interest that with the masses shift from objective to objective. Here mundane astrology has its day by identifying these movements in the thoughts of man with the periods of the great planets. The sudden inventive wave, the higher criticism and metaphysically speculative years, the general fad and cult prominence, the strenuous age, the day of the efficiency man, the flapper-jazz period all are charted as easily by the astrologer as the more tangible phe-

[1]Cf. p. 36.

nomena of the mineral and vegetable kingdoms are classified by the physical scientist.

Rebirth of the human conscious principle is a fear-inspiring stumbling-block to the modern mind. Yet perennials do not disturb the botanist though the tulip returns with its shape and color in response to the same natural law which rules consciousness. The language of the street recognizes a sort of reincarnation since it terms a man a Nero, a Napoleon or some lesser neighborhood character. That the individual cannot recollect prior experiences is no case in point. The tulip remembers nothing while man himself can recall only scattered incidents of his early years and those hazily and inaccurately. Memory is a matter of mental development. A broad general public belief in reincarnation is unimportant to occult philosophy.[1]

All activity, substance and form thus first approach understanding through the time perspectives which are achieved by domain or sphere of substance and by cycle or repetition in activity and by reduplication in form.

[1]The restrictions upon public instruction in higher metaphysics by all occult teachers of authority are not a matter of monopoly of truth since no earnest student has ever been denied and Pythagoras who was quite a flighty Greek was able to obtain entrance to the high temple of the very particular Egyptian hierarchy at a time when the mysteries were about to be sealed in preparation for a new cycle. Rather it is recognition of the long and very difficult special training necessary for the layman who seeks knowledge widely removed both from his experience and from his ability for useful employment of it in human society. Only the charlatan tantalizes the general mass with fascinating half-truths far beyond untrained comprehension.

THE WARP-THREAD IN POINT OF VIEW

Knowledge is wholly a matter of perspective. The esotericism claimed by many misguided devotees of mystic philosophy does not exist. The relationship which inheres through all things puts into the hands of any seeker a path to understanding that cannot be closed to him even did higher intelligences so will. The human brain must be trained to receive any sort of specialized knowledge whether metaphysical or otherwise. In the terms of occult philosophy this mental development is enlargement of consciousness or a broadening to include in point of view greater domains or wider and deeper cycles.

The path to illumination is an organization of this process. The method is used by modern science and was employed in the ancient mysteries. The investigator through attentuation or disassociation merely separates some simple fact or process thoroughly known to him and then builds upon it.

Errors of understanding in modern gnosis come from reassociation and from carelessness in the definition of terms but never from the starting point taken. Too frequently a student seeks to grasp whole a matter which fills the mind of God. The seeker who has no time for small and petty matters fails to remember that the most perfect representation of the universe is that basic tiny atom upon which all substance and being are built. A watch requires more skillful workmanship than a clock and a minature greater physical skill with brush and pigment than a full sized portrait.

A perspective, point of view or starting place is necessary for all analysis. In occultism the cycles or arcs of perspective are taken one by one through the various domains whenever and wherever a cross-section of observation may be obtained. The keys to knowledge used by the occultist are based upon this principle.[1] Not only does direct investigation and observation contribute to occult knowledge of time but all the tabulated facts and demonstrations of geology, history, zoology, embryology, botany and allied sciences of growth and succession prove and disprove the occult hypotheses.

The thread of perspective must be seen as the warp through the weft of the fabric of knowledge. This process is served in the analysis of duration by the key truth that time is illusion.

NUMBER AS A DEPOSITORY OF KNOWLEDGE

The Pythagorean numerical basis of wisdom possesses an odd attraction to occult students and has been the foundation of arcane teaching through many centuries. Similarly the seven rays of cosmic emanation and the eight active schools of divine wisdom lend fascination to modern metaphysical research.

The Pythagorean numbers are the fundamental types of cosmic expression. The seven divine rays

[1]For the keys to knowledge cf. p. 181 ff.

with the one that never emanates provide the eight
schools which are manifest. These are not organizations but are a classification of the human approaches to understanding. The schools correlate
to the numbers.

The first number is no-number. It is the Pythagorean cipher, zero or oudad.[1] Here is the annihilative principle in nature or a fundamental reversion underlying all creation. Undifferentiated cosmic
substance is that chaos which is known only through
time or the eternity of faith and of conventional
philosophy. As substance it has no being, form
or activity. But because it is the repository of all
things and the invisible space-filling ocean from
which all sprang and to which all will return it is
that eternal duration out of which any time measure
however vast is but an impermanent subdivision.

The first school is the Absolute[2] or the non-techni-
cal faith-born identification of all things in that inclusive reality which has no identity. It is the conquest of difficulty by transcendence and is the practical use and application in daily affairs of the principles which are founded in time perspective. It
denies the limitation of duration and so of space
or condition. Founded in America in the New

[1] A word without dictionary authority and the equivalent of zero
in the series monad, duad, triad, etc.

[2] These general names given the schools are arbitrary and a matter of convenience. Here is no necessary connection with several
philosophies which employ the capitalized term Absolute while a
similarly general usage follows in the cases of Unity, Rosicrucian
and Theosophy. Cf. foot-note p. 9.

England transcendentalism it has had its vast growth in New Thought or the general Metaphysical movement and in Christian Science.

For the modern world the prophet is Mary Baker G. Eddy.[1] It is to Christian Science and its founder that America most owes the present wide-spread toleration of a divine concept which was startling and revolutionary to the lay mind in the eighteen-nineties. She spoke splendidly for that which a scientific occultism conveniently classifies as the philosophy of the oudad or first school.

---

[1]The eight prophets represent no attempt to set up an occult hall of fame. Many of the most valuable workers and pioneers are slighted as here in the instance of Emerson and Quimby. A prophet in the literal meaning of the word is one who speaks for another and the result desired through this arbitrary selection is the identification of the individual in each case who most closely interprets the genius of his particular school to the largest and widest audience. The matter of the sources and motives of Mrs. Eddy does not enter into the consideration. Neither is the occult philosopher concerned with her methods or with any possible superior excellence of other earlier or later expressions in the teaching of the oudad.

CHAPTER II

THE PERSPECTIVE OF LIFE IN SPACE

SPACE IS RELATIONSHIP

THE second key truth is important because it is distributive. Immediately following the achievement of a sense in all mass of an illusion or impermanence increasing in direct proportion to the distance away from everlasting cosmic reality the occult seeker must learn that through the myriad recapitulative and cyclic activities of being and substance is found a pattern of interwoven cooperative relationship which holds even the outermost shred of independent matter in constant and eternal unity with the ultimate. All things are related to all other things in activity, substance and form.

Creation is a springing forth of undifferentiated root-stuff from darkness and chaos into objective being. In the physical realm this is a complete separation from the cosmic source of all. But space itself is not separation nor is it even the whole of creation in the sense of a visible and invisible reality brought out of nothing. Rather it is relationship or

61

the sum of universal cooperations. It is the position of anything relative to all things. As time or duration is a support and limitation of being so also is space to the same degree but in a different manner. Duration is the foundation and space the means of existence.

Space is never substance but is rather the situation or placing of form and being in the matrix of duration. It is not the extent of the universe but is instead a cosmic quality. It is as truly a fundamental dimension as time. The occult conception of space permits a perspective out upon all creation from any convenient center and this is a possibility which is the demonstration for the universality of the hypothesis.

Space as merely the abstract possibility of extension in the conventional use of the word permits an infinity beyond knowledge which is foreign to occultism. No supersensual philosophy is satisfactory unless it offers an explanation for every known form, process and phenomenon. A space boundless yet cognizable and actual in substance and activity is an intellectual morass in which any understanding must soon bog itself. The apparent infinity of the universe is space but is not substance. Space is the coordination of sensual impressions of heavenly bodies and all other cosmic extensions of mundane matter and property. It is pure or abstract relationship.

THE OCCULT NATURE OF SPACE

The foundation of the occult hypothesis of space is the sphere or basic globular form of matter marked in the atom, in simple cellular types of lower life and in the heavenly bodies. Mathematically and philosophically the whole structure of occultism is built upon the sphere.

The familiar Hermetic axiom "As above, so below" is the popular statement of an ancient understanding of interdependent mundane and cosmic spheres with the smaller situated in the center of the larger and with the outer surface of the one reflecting and duplicating the inner surface of the other. The original doctrine of seven heavens or twelve cosmic regions was a hypothesis of concentrically situated spheres and while at one stage of human knowledge these realms became domes capping a flat earth yet even in this error is every indication of an early grasp of occult truth.

In supersensual mathematics the sphere doctrine becomes astrology.

The apparently revolving heavens are divided into geometric mansions by the trisection of quadrants formed in the extension to the celestial vault of the zenith and horizon meridians from any point upon the globe. These mansions are the houses of astrological nomenclature. They reflect the influence of the earth sphere into the cosmos. Similarly the celestial vault is divided into another twelve mansions through quadrants taken at the equinoxes and solstices and trisected by meridians containing the axis of the ecliptic or that exact path of the earth which lies in the approximate plane of the orbits of all members of the solar system. These are the signs of the zodiac through which is found any reflection of cosmic influence into individual or mundane matters.

In common practice astrology is thought to be a matter of actual stellar influence but such a doctrine is untenable and is responsible for the universal rejection of astrology by modern scientific minds. The fixed zodiac measured from the vernal equinox is the basis of unchanged astrological delineation through more than twenty-five hundred years of written record.[1] In this period the constellations have moved more than the space of a zodiacal sign through the heavens.

The fact that the planets indicate an influence but do not send it out through their rays[2] is thoroughly obvious to the competent student predicting from a horoscope. The actual planetary positions at any period of life are least influential in a nativity[3] while for the thirtieth year as an example the positions a

[1] In the Bible beginning with the book of Ezekiel whose authorship is assigned by practically all critics to the sixth century B.C. and particularly continuing in Daniel which is a book given by conservative scholars no later a date than the first century before Christ.

[2] Planetary influence is taught as such because it is the simplest method or that device of symbolism known as metonymy.

[3] Transits or ephemeris position.

month following birth[1] are much more powerful and
aspects formed two hours after birth[2] are most
potent of all. This is a matter of occult geometry
in the interchange of time measure which underlies
the first key truth and in that analysis of all phenomena and matter by the unvarying cosmic relationships of philosophical space with which the second key truth is concerned.

The clue to this understanding of space in occult
philosophy is through the universal gravitation of
Newton. Natural law is immutable. Force and
matter are indestructible. Activity, substance and
chemical form may change and indeed these undergo
constant transmutation in regular cycles of growth
or decay. The attraction which draws an apple to
the ground keeps the earth in orderly movement
through the solar system. The occultist only steps
beyond Newton in the application of universal gravitation to consciousness. Science gives no logical
reason for excepting sentient phenomena from natural law.

Spherical geometry is the mathematics of divinity.
Through the astrological resolution of form into its
integral parts is gained scientific understanding of
the myriad complexities in the make-up of vehicles
in sentient life. This astrological process reveals
the odd persistence of pattern in objective mani-

[1]Secondary directions or the Arabian system commonly used.

[2]Primary directions or the Placidian system seldom employed by
modern astrologers because a considerable amount of patience and
mathematical competency is required.

festations of being even to the uttermost attenuation of form and function.

A true science of occultism lies beyond the present introductory analysis of philosophical fundamentals. As sentient life is built upon the sphere in the simple organic cell, cosmic constitution upon the same globe form in the heavenly bodies, matter itself upon the atom or chemical molecule so is occult philosophy built entirely upon spherical conceptions.

Linear distance is the most useless dimension in any domain of human investigation. With the conquest of time in modern invention all objective separation has been annihilated. And truly a youthful swain may be much further away from a young lady beside him on a sofa than from the less charming custodian of his heart thousands of miles away in the antipodes. In heavenly mathematics the physical scientist alone is interested by the light-years of distance. The occultist has gained spherical consciousness and for him nothing exists except in terms of relationship.

The occultist learns from experience what the child often wise in its grasp of antecedent divinity knows instinctively and as a matter of course. Anything which intrudes into the consciousness idly should be pushed aside. All that seems in any way related to the matter at hand is important.

The sphere is not only the type of basic form but is also the symbol of occult coordination. Every part is equally in relationship to the center. The sphere in a sense exists because of its core. All differentiation of matter has being in a nucleus of inception. No understanding of anything is found without a center.

Astronomy has been much confused for lack of a doctrine of nuclei. Copernicus gave the world a heliocentric knowledge which the ancients possessed but lost in simple disinterest and now modern science is beginning to rediscover the geocentric system. While it is true that the earth travels about the sun yet the reverse is the apparent fact and it is from apparent facts that real knowledge is gained. Therefore astrology is geocentric.[1]

The situation of an observer materially affects his deductions. July is winter to an Argentinian. He may philosophically understand it to be summer in America but to him it remains winter nevertheless. The phenomenon of the rising and setting of the sun is life to mankind. That this is brought about by the motion of the earth itself is important to the occultist or philosopher but man existed successfully before he knew it. Today men live better as they dwell first in simple truths or in matters which may be actual in their own experience.

The sense of the illusion in lower things is built upon a conquest of grosser reality. This is not a denial but is rather a sympathetic understanding. The fiction of the stork or of Santa Claus does no

[1]A heliocentric astrology exists and within narrow bounds is very successful though merely a translation of geocentric coordinates.

harm to childish minds and even in adult belief could hardly appear more foolish than the modern biologically sophisticated youngster.

Man is the center of any sphere known to him. Any effort on his part to transpose his focus of consciousness as a particular sphere's center to a point without his being and beyond his experience leads to confusion. Because the human being possesses imagination he is able with a growth in understanding of natural law to draw accurate deductions from a point wide of his own self-consciousness yet even in this case the result is accomplished by a paralleling of experience which is a phenomenon of occult space mastery and which involves no more than an interchange of relationship factors in the manner of the transposition of time units.

In life man stands the center of many realms. All activity, substance and form are the result of that spherical constitution in relationship which is the occult nature of space. The tendency of physical form to curves, arcs and properties of the circle is commonly observed. Substance is made up of chemical aggregations of atoms which are globular in shape. Being itself begins in the cell or the egg and expands in consciousness which in its spread is aura-like and avoid. Even the material vocabulary of every-day affairs symbolizes a trained man as well-rounded.

The spheres of creation in gradation of realm are philosophically concentric. Man is an atom in the vehicle[1] of a god from whom his inner flame is an offthrown spark. Similarly each human individual is divine to all the cells which constitute his physical structure and so to them by virtue of their presence in his body he gives higher being and a lesser spark of divinity. The earth reflects the entire universe of which it is a tiny atom and also contains a cosmos of its own in chemical molecules. The atom itself is thought by science to hold a tiny solar system.

As time units are interchangeable so are these basic denominators of space dimension. Here is the doctrine of macrocosm and microcosm or of great world and little universe in a cosmic man and a human cosmos. In the individual are all the elements of stellar being and in the heavens the reflection of each separate faculty of man. Everything is dimension. This is space and space is relationship.

In terms of process the relationship is subjectivity while in terms of situation it is objectivity.

The constant and eternal unity of all with the ultimate center results from the interplay of these two space factors. First is the indestructible force which as activity works invisibly and yet reveals itself in a human mood or in a star dissolved to dust thousands of light-years distant and which is termed subjectivity. Second is the visible matter which forms and decays in constant response to underlying cause and

---

[1]Vehicle is used synonymously with body in this treatise but with somewhat greater technical distinction. An individual incarnate possesses several bodies which are vehicles for his principles.

so permits the manifestation of substance and form in that crystallization of being which is objectivity.[1]

Distance and size are qualities as fundamentally illusionary as conventional time.

PERSPECTIVES OF LIFE IN SPACE

Primer instruction in space consciousness is gained through the occult cosmogony and anthropogeny[2] in the manner that first instruction in cycles and time transcendence is received intellectually through astrology. The birth and evolution of the globe as a unit in a universal scheme is reflected in the smaller process of the beginning of human life manifestation and the growth of man upon the earth.

The first perspective of life in space must be sought through the largest physical unit susceptible to sensual contact by man. This is the planet on which he dwells. At the outset all being must be analyzed through the globe itself. Here is the physical sphere shared by man and each member of the lower orders in sentient evolution. Upon the earth and constituting its structure is the chemical sub-

---

[1]Here in objectivity and subjectivity begins the detailed construction of occult operative concepts embodied in single words upon the analogy of time, space, etc. Cf. foot-note p. 39 and note particularly the employment of single words to express the aspects in Appendix A, p. 254.

[2]Of generally accepted occult works *The Secret Doctrine,* H. P. Blavatsky (2 vols., London 1888), is the most voluminous gathering of metaphysical tradition in commentary upon current materialistic hypotheses while *The Rosicrucian Cosmo-Conception,* Max Heindel (Seattle 1909), is the most lucid outline of the whole superphysical scheme of periods, globes, epochs and races and of the worlds, planes, vehicles and faculties of man.

stance out of which spring all forms of life from the very simple to the extremely complex. Matter may and does change its nature but in its substance it is indestructible and except for infinitesimal gain or loss through meteoric phenomena it is wholly confined to the globe. The orders of being vary in function and situation upon the earth but they have been transplanted frequently from one to another terrestrial location and condition. No shred of competent evidence is available for a belief in a transfer of physical substance or objective sentient life either from one planet to another or from the solar system out to foreign stars and to other constellations of the visible universe. Yet no proof is found of essential limitation in any amount of interchange in activity, substance or form throughout the earth's own sphere.

The globe is the perfect example of cosmic unity and so it becomes a convenient basic dimension unit in space.

Between the various activities harbored within its realm exists a perfect cooperation. The same chemical laws underlie inorganic and sentient phenomena. Many of the carbon compounds of living organism can now be produced synthetically in the laboratory and with the growth of adequate knowledge all will be at will. Plant and animal tissues are merely built upon specializations of inorganic matter. Mineral decay produces life-giving soil fertility while organic decomposition provides the basis of coal which is the most useful and diamond which is the most valuable product of inorganic crystallization. The living plant and the breathing animal are mutually interdependent through an alchemy of respiration and metabolism by which the excretions of the one are vitally necessary for the other. Any complex sentient structure both feeds upon and nourishes more simple form and this is a globe-wide process which marks the completeness of the sphere's self-containment.

Universality or spiritual citizenship is identified with the globe as a whole. World thinkers are commonly accounted to be those who refuse to accept limitations of land, race or established creed. The first step beyond the stage of tribal deity in the divine consciousness of man was the conception of a religion to span the continents and of a god alike the property of every human individual. The story of Jonah who went aboard ship to escape the Jewish god seems ridiculous in modern times. Internationalism with all its peculiar bigotry and its avoidance of civilized obligation is yet reaching out for this great cosmic oneness.

The second perspective of life in space deals with the limitation of divine unity upon the earth and with the various illuminating differences in objective form and activity which are thereby produced. This is analysis by continent or geographical geometry.

A continent to the conventionalist is a very set punctuation of eternal oceans by accidental splashes of land upon which a haphazard evolution of sentient life has taken place. Unfortunately for the peace of those disturbed by thought of cataclysm the researches of geology have demonstrated thoroughly a sporadic rise and fall of all lands. Scientific investigation has yielded rather perfect proof of Lemuria[1] through the wide distribution of related flora and fauna and has provided a not inconsiderable demonstration of the Atlantis named in ancient tradition.[2]

Occultism knows that a given area of land through its position and constitution has a definite distributive effect and specializes the evolutionary processes taking place upon its surface. This understanding gives a sense of order and purpose in space dimension.

People in particular are seen to be vastly modified by their place of settlement. Language is observed to change and to grow in its center but to stand still if carried elsewhere by a colony of men who cling to their mother tongue. Thus Revolutionary-period English of a strikingly perfect sort is found among isolated mountaineers in the United States. The French of Canada speak the tongue which marks the period of their emigration. Yet America does not use British or true English and the original Latin has become several Romance languages.

[1]The name given by conventional science and accepted by occultism.

[2]In Plato's *Timaeus* and *Critias*. In occult philosophy the island of Plato is known as Poseidonis. It was the last surviving remnant of the once vast Atlantean continent.

Similarly social habits change and physical form modifies itself in reference to centers of influence. In the blending of racial streams North-American blood absorbs Jewish while South-American Spanish blood accepts Indian and Negro without revulsion. These are results impossible in older lands. Investigation shows even a noticeable difference in the type and contour of heads when children are born of the same parents in Europe and in North America.

The materialist states that this is due to climate. The occult philosopher understands that climate itself is an additional result of the continental factor. Science has rediscovered the intimate association between weather and vegetation and has found that each controls the other. The biologist begins to believe that nothing in nature is truly useless or wholly destructive. The fine delicate inner balance between all normal phenomena upon the earth is but reflection in a small field of cosmic equilibrium established through the broad general relationship of space dimension.

The obliquity of the ecliptic or angle of inclination between the plane of the earth's orbit and the plane of its rotation is the mathematical basis of the continental factor. Anthropologists have attributed to mere accident the consistent and principal development of inhabitable land upon the northern hemisphere. Only astrology has the explanation since in the southern half of the sphere the zodiacal rulerships of the important centers in the body are thrown under short ascension.[1] Below the equator are decadent racial remnants and very youthful and virile type beginnings. Towards the south man's development is thrown out of balance so that in time a normal race destroys itself. Not since the obliquity exceeded one hundred and eighty degrees in reference to the present position and not since the sun rose in the west and set in the east has life shown an appreciable development upon the southern hemisphere.

The third perspective is by country and nation. Country provides the tempering areas of civilization, culture and breeding. Nations and national subdivisions set up associations in group macrospheres of mass consciousness.

The fourth perspective is by microsphere or the individual situation in consciousness through family, health, talent and cooperation with other individuals.

Here particularly is indicated the process of whittling down point of view in that attenuation which must mark the investigation of occult science. Space relationships as well as time units are interchangeable.

The countries or nations and the continents mutually interpret one another. A citizen of the United States is called an American. A Britisher or Frenchman in his points of view explains Europe while

[1]Signs of short ascension rise more swiftly and fewer people are born with their influence placed upon the ascendent and mid-heaven.

the term continental aptly phrases that tolerance of individual thought which is to be found in France or Germany but which is almost wholly missing in the United States.

An individual represents a family, a community, a nation or a continent. In astrology a chart of the heavens may be read for the immediate subject or his blood relatives and for his acquired associates as marriage or business partners and offspring. Such is possible only because a fine network of interwoven influence exists through all creation. So certain is this reflexive interchange that a municipality or a nation cannot acquire or select a ruler or head but that the horoscope of that individual at once serves to indicate the forces at work in the larger group. From these charts of national leaders predictions are made with remarkable accuracy.[1]

These are perspectives of life in space through unity which is complete and self-sufficient but yet serves as a part of successively superior units in greater schemes and through unity whose subdivisions are themselves units complete and self-sufficient within their own activities and realms.

The sphere is understood philosophically and mathematically through its center. For consciousness a focal point must be found and for anything a

[1]The astrologers of neutral America in 1914 predicted Central Power defeat from the Kaiser's horoscope with the single exception of a professor in Los Angeles who used an experimental method and another in Hoboken who bore a German name.

nucleus from which perspective is taken. Relationship in occult philosophy is identified by the transposition of units. Space denominators interchange
through identity of center.[1] In any convenient center
may be found the basic unity of all.[2]

THE OCCULT ANALYSIS OF DIMENSION

The practical organization of space conception
in occult philosophy is through emphasis of the distinction between objective and subjective phenomena.

All that is supersensual is subjective to ordinary
consciousness. Yet primary gradations of subjective
realms must exist and the first organization must be
by abstract dimension or by perspective of higher
space in the cooperative relations which are not directly traceable through objective reactions and results.

Higher space is a broadly general term of no practical value. It includes those things which may only
be understood fully by philosophical dimension.
Among these are the objective expressions of human
consciousness such as sleep, dreams, imagination,
mental creation or superphysical phenomena following upon abnormal development of the senses and
also the subjective activities of consciousness itself
such as intuition, prescience or purely psychic mani-

[1]The mathematical explanation of the use of a ruler's horoscope
for a nation.
[2]Cf. p. 84. This is a philosophical explanation of the Christian
teaching that the kingdom of heaven is within each individual.
For the necessary spiritual focal center cf. p. 124 and foot-note[2] p.
238.

festation. Philosophies and abstruse mathematical achievements have their birth in conceptions of the abstract mind of man. Revelation of the divine or any similar enlarged world vision exists through the mental matrix which functions within the higher space of superphysical relationship.

But a sense of higher dimension rather than a definition of higher space must be taken as a foundation for the space conception of occultism. In the achievement of this the match-box demonstration is useful despite its play upon the term right-angle.

A point is taken at a corner of the box. This is the dot or a mathematical concept imagined to be without length, breadth or thickness. If this dot is extended away from itself in any direction the operation produces a line or the first dimension which is situated at right angles to no-dimension and is represented by any edge of the box. If next this line is extended away from itself in any direction the operation produces a plane or the second dimension which is situated at right angles to the first and also to no-dimension and is represented by any side of the box. The plane is bounded by lines and the lines by dots. The line mathematically has neither breadth nor thickness while the plane lacks only the latter. If now the plane is extended away from itself on either side it gains thickness and so evolves the third dimension in a solid situated at right angles to all prior dimensions and bounded by all the dots, lines and planes or represented by the match-box as it stands.

In this demonstration the principal point is that all dimensions include those which go before and that in the case of each those higher are indefinable in its own terms and are only to be described as situated at the hypothetical right angles or in projection away and out from the known into the unknown.

For the fourth dimension a quality is needed bounded by the dots, lines, planes and solidity of the box. This is an unknown something at right angles to all measurable conceptions. In a sense it is the transcendence of time and space which has so far been the entire subject of this treatise. The observer figuratively is situated inside the box with universal vision as though he possessed eyes also back, above, below and on both sides of him so that he could thus see every side, edge and corner of the box in one coordinate view. If the box is broken open and flattened out it gives a faint approximation of this result.

In common human consciousness a perfect but generally shadowlike fourth-dimensional faculty is found in visual imagination. A single word will conjure up an inner picture of some familiar place. As recreated within the mind this image has a fourth-dimensional tendency to be seen or sensed in its entirety rather than as last viewed by physical sight. The mind is accustomed to the limitation of the eye and reduces the mental picture to a familiar aspect. But this projection in point of view through the fourth dimension is the faculty developed into astral clairvoyance and it may be cultivated by deliberate exercise.

Fourth-dimensional consciousness is important as a type of space realization and it is peculiarly a human attribute. It leads to a simple understanding of gradation in subjective realms.

Inert or invisible matter corresponds to no-dimension. As first specialized in the mineral kingdom it is inactive and is responsive to one dimension only or to motion.[1] By a secondary specialization of chemical atoms in the vegetable kingdom a life principle is added so that substance drawn in or thrown off through the first dimension of action and reaction in straight motion lines is responsive to the second dimension which may then be called expansion or simple growth. In animals this matter is active in vegetablelike or growth constitution but it is responsive to a third dimension which is being[2] in objective substance through material self-consciousness and which gives first independence of movement upon the physical three-dimensional sphere. Man in the terms of occult philosophy is more than animal. He

[1]This is basic cosmic force or the emanative or simple reflex tendency that is not to be confused with the intelligence or instinct which motion outwardly represents.

[2]Being as the widest possible category is possessed by mineral and vegetable kingdoms but as a quality of existence it is most strongly focused in the three-dimensional realm where expression is solid and is given in the greatest and most considerable degree to the animal nature.

is constituted in physical self-consciousness or being but is responsive to the fourth dimension which is the abstract quality of form[1] or supersensual responsibility for objective relationship. Man alone is a creator and alone can project his point of view or his experience into things outside his being. His thoughts become plans and these by himself or other men are clothed in actuality. While an animal is baffled by a wall of tissue paper a Columbus sails out upon unknown oceans through the faith of imagination.

In space analysis by dimension each domain of conscious expression is limited by that dimension above the one to which it is responsive. The higher dimension in each case becomes a subjective realm to the objectivity of lower constitution. Perspective is carried on into higher spheres by development of consciousness or by analogy and in this manner the realms of the subjective are charted. Any distinction between objective and subjective is found to be wholly relative while the clue to subjective understanding remains in objective identification by aspect.[2]

The second organization of occult space conception is by form because the control of types through an understanding of abstract pattern is the mastery of that dimension of consciousness in which the human being is outwardly responsive.

[1]Archetypes or thought-forms in conventional occultism.
[2]Cf. Appendix A, p. 254.

In dealing with form the occultist demands a constant emphasis of the objective for both analysis and perspective and so he ignores the supersensual. His interest is in the division of forms into types and the tendency of types to persist or to display regular modification.

In sentient form he is concerned with kingdoms, races and species and with their eccentricities as well as their orderly development. Normal manifestation of life discloses itself in a persistence of pattern[1] which reveals the inner coordinations while eccentricity uncovers the deeper and wider relationships in all life and being. Through chemical form is traced out the differentiation or the specialization by elemental constitution of primordial underlying root substance. Here in crystallization is revealed that form tendency which is the extreme of variation from the fundamental sphere and which in occult tradition is the ultimate chemical crystal built in response to all force. To mystics this is known as the philosopher's stone or spirit-cut diamond of a myriad facets.[2]

The third organization of occult space conception is by activity or by emphasis of subjective phenomena through cycles. This involves chemical change and also the habits, tendencies and temperament to be

[1]The strides in modern surgery have been possible only through the dissection of cadavers. Even the slightest deviation in the human pattern is rare.

[2]Form is the entire consideration of the key truth and chapter following this, p. 87 ff.

discovered in all sentient life. As form wherever found is significant in its similarity and dissimilarity to all other form whether sentient or otherwise so activity is comparable to activity. Here is the practical application of astrology to superphysical research.

The guiding principles in the whole of scientific occult investigation of relationship are found through abstract dimension. By these principles all space conceptions are organized.

SPIRITUALITY AND SPACE CONSCIOUSNESS

The non-philosopher finds extreme difficulty in any realization that spirituality is relative. Yet divine awareness is purely a matter of space consciousness.

In the ancient mysteries the method of spiritual development was no more than an induction of enlarged cosmic understanding whether by use of numbers, symbols and secret histories or by actual psychic training. Religious ecstasy is a phallic catalysis which awakens consciousness in dormant sense centers of the body and in corresponding higher vehicles. The rites of alcoholic and sexual stimulation in religions of the past were frank but otherwise did not differ greatly in terms of space consciousness from the methods of a modern Christian revival. In some present-day occult groups physical intoxication for astral growth is still employed as in the practise of sex communion or intimacy without orgasm. Growth through negation of sensual impulse and appetite or through repression is a reversed method of phallic catalysis which excites spiritual reflex through mental self-approval and is a method generally accepted by modern schools though it differs from earlier means only in a greater safety to the individual.

Man is the center of the universe. To the extent that he is able to induce or create spheres of consciousness from his focus of being out to include wider and greater sweeps of understanding and influence to that extent does he grow into the ultimate and the divine. The seeker who senses the things of God is himself god. The kingdom of heaven is within because its center must be set up by the individual. Beyond are many mansions in which an aspirant may dwell but all are concentric and are built upon himself.

Illusion supports itself in time and also in space. Spheres may be shared by many souls but each will know and understand only those realms which he can draw through occult geometry about his own center of being.

"One single world, one single soul, one single God," said Hermes long before our era. "As above, so below; in all things unity!"

NUMERICAL RELATIONSHIP

The second number is all-number, the Pythagorean one or monad.[1]

[1]Monad as here used refers to the occult nature or essential

In its completeness it carries the oudad with it and becomes the decad or ten. The decad is the consolidation principle in nature or the final conscious reacceptance of differentiation in unity. The monad is the first emanation of force and impulse through the basic cooperation of all activity, substance and form in purpose. It reinforces creation in a constant emanation of first principle. It supports the succeeding numbers which contain it and at the end receives all other numbers back again into its own self because it has never ceased or diminished.

The monad is motion and is eternal and constant force. Out of the primordial emanation all further differentiation is evolved and so the one is the first and the last.

The second school is Unity or philosophic Christianity. "I and my Father are one," said the Nazarene.[1] "No man cometh unto the Father but by me."[2] This is spiritual unity because of identity in centers of consciousness. This is the doctrine of intercession and of vicarious atonement because here is a drawing of centers together in oneness of relationship until the separation of illusion is transcended in space as well as in time.

Space is relationship. Spiritual development is unity.

principle of the number one and must not be confused with the Theosophical employment of the word for the individual divine spark or ego atom.

[1]John, 10:30. [2]John, 14:6.

The prophet is St. John the Divine who is the author[1] of the Fourth Gospel. Through his dramatization of the mission of Christ and through the words of the gentle master placed by him in a definite philosophical scheme the beloved disciple laid the foundation of a great world religion of compassion and brotherhood and gave a key to the greatest of the inner truths taught these Galilean disciples. In John's name a world devout in intention has preserved and has publicly accepted the fountain principles of the monad through almost two millenia.

[1]The moot question of actual authorship of the gospel is unimportant since the contents and not the traditional authority are valuable to the occult philosopher. It is merely convenient to accept as author the companion of Christ.

CHAPTER III

THE DOMAINS OF FORM

FORM IS BALANCE

HE third key truth is important because it is comparative. Through all being lies a pattern of interwoven cooperative relations. No part of creation stands alone in the universe. All things are related to all other things in activity, substance and form.

For the first step in tracing out various schemes or orders of cooperation in time and space the supersensual philosopher turns to form as the most objective and most conveniently studied product of the forces and processes active through natural law. Everything that has being is individual and independent within its own sphere. This individuality reflects itself and best displays its signatures through objective constitution because the crystallization that determines form is a process which in its very independence of nature is furthest removed from primordial unity and from ultimate cosmic reassociation.

Likenesses common to the most divergent forms are of greatest use to the investigator. The presence of the vermiform appendix in the wombat since that Australian marsupial stands low in the evolutionary scale of mammals is a clue to the never-ceasing chance given stragglers in all processes of growth. The appendix is the tiny physiological mark of humanity.[1]   Found in the anthropoid apes it verifies the occult teaching that these primates are not a type of animals near the man stage but rather are laggard race remnants that once were men.   The wombat is the present degeneracy of forms which were human when the present humanity of the planet Venus dwelt upon this earth.[2]   So long as these egos possess forms they may yet turn and evolve forward. In this instance a perspective of opportunity is increased by millions of years.

Similarly the presence of attracting or repelling colors and odors in vegetable and animal kingdoms is of scientific interest but the special faculty of the animal organism to display quick change both of color and of odor in response to emotion as the blush or reddened eye and as the strange cloying passion perfume on the breath or disagreeable accentuation of perspiration upon fright or anger gives the occultist a clue of supreme importance.   He quickly recognizes a vegetable principle raised to higher power within and subordinate to the outer animal

[1]Not to be confused with an elongated or sacculated caecum as in some of the rodents.

[2]The Pandean life-stream in occult philosophy.   Cf. foot-notes pp. 99[2], 245[2].

form of man and beast.   He identifies this as the
etheric double of occultism.

Form is balance because it is a natural opposite
in the pendulum swing of tendency towards and
away from an inherent divine constitution.   Form
marks the pause following the operation of forces
of crystallization into objective responsible being
and preceding the processes of dissolution by which
the structure itself decays.   It is a hesitancy in which
inner being or consciousness has greatest opportunity to exert its fullest measure of independence and
individuality since in objective form lies the ultimate
of separation from the eternal.   Visible creation or
the tangible world is the testing ground and the
proving field of consciousness in matter.   Form is
the balance from which progress may be spiritual
and upward or may be terrestrial and through smaller and narrower cycles of recapitulation deeper and
downward into further and more separative crystallization as seen in the odd little lost Australian Venus-
man or in the Lemurian stragglers[1] embodied as anthropoid apes.

Form is balance because it is the interlocking in
temporary objective pattern of the creative force and
responsible impulse that must work through every
cooperative domain concerned in being.   The fine-
ness of this balance in the structure of man is commonly observed in medical practice through which
the tiniest drug stimulation may sometimes be used

[1]Cf. foot-note[1] p. 233.

with appreciable result while in other cases a whole apothecary shop may be administered piecemeal without noticeable effect. In the activity of human moods a single idea may possess inductive power sufficient to cause an invalid of years to leap to his feet with health or else to send an otherwise normal and virile man to bed helpless from acute physical pain. These contrasts are not miracles nor astonishing phenomena but are merely instances of external cooperation with tendencies which already are powerful. The occultist who knows the human form and who possesses the skill to read symptoms in terms of their coordinate rulerships may with predetermined certainty accomplish as great results either through simple stimulation or through repercussion in the case of centers and functions that cannot be reached directly.

Mastery of form follows an understanding of the domains of balance.

THE OCCULT CONCEPTION OF DOMAIN

In his conception of domains the occult philosopher adds little to science beyond breadth in point of view. The materialist resents the coordination of mental state to bodily ill while the psychoanalyst instinctively feels cheated by epidemics and by cyclic types of disease which cannot be traced to his fascinating realm of the subconscious. Each of these extremists deals with truth in his own narrow bounds of limitation. The occultist must consider both extremes and also all intermediary views. He must recognize the fact that emphasis in an individual case may occur in material or in psychic and other realms. He must understand that no correct diagnosis can be made until the point of consciousness or the focus of condition is identified.

Domain itself by occult definition is the limitation in cycle of activity by a boundary of form type. Articulate sound requires a breathing organism and all faculty a foundation in form. From the general and obvious signatures which may be instanced in the great class of beings known as the animal kingdom down to the fine and subtle distinctions of species and groups within the animal domain itself form undergoes a constant specialization and adaptation to function that indicates to the supersensual scientist the forces and influences at work and active. Similar gradations mark the human and the lower kingdoms.

Through domain occult philosophy establishes the basic groups of life sparks[1] and sentient egos. Life-stream is the occult technical term for the community of entities of being within the boundaries of domain. Man is the human life-stream and in other spheres are other human waves which have been or will be active on the present planet. Upon the earth all men belong to one life-stream because the

[1]The ego is the immaterial enduring self and the evolving and improving or else degenerating principle of separation while the divine or life spark is the eternal cosmic germ which never loses unity with the first cause and so is termed the individual absolute.

globe itself provides the boundary of form type and so establishes this particular domain.[1]   Similarly the animal, vegetable and mineral types designate domains upon the planet.   When occult philosophy advances into purely supersensual realms as in an investigation of Rosicrucian elemental spirits it discovers other domains not considered here but subject to the same principles and the same space relationships.   Heaven worlds do not rise above natural law but provide larger domains in wider spheres.   The Christian angels borrowed from the Persian ray of wisdom are no more than members of a normal life-stream known to occult philosophy as the subempyrean.

Kingdom is the general technical term for the collection of objective forms of the life-stream active in the domain which the kingdom identifies.   Form itself becomes the balance in crystallization of the objective and subjective forces or tendencies induced and engendered through the life-stream entities which make up any particular kingdom.

A conception of domain peculiar to occult philosophy is the inclusion by activity as well as by presence of all lower general form types or kingdoms in those higher and more composite in construction.[2]   Science knows that the mineral chemical atoms make up the higher life types and to the materialist these

[1]For the apparent exception cf. foot-note[1] p. 241.
[2]This is the doctrine of vehicles found in nearly all conventional occult teaching. Cf. p. 150 ff.

complex evolved forms are no more than mineral substance chemically superactive. In a sense the material view here is closely akin to that of occult philosophy. The occultist teaches that mineral atoms taken into vegetable or animal forms are undergoing additional specialization and are more active than if placed in inorganic composition. But this additional activity still is taking place within the mineral domain and is a matter of fundamental vibration or chemical process only.

The fact that mineral atoms lie in superior forms means that greater activity is thereby induced within them. The genesis and being of higher life result from factors different and apart from the chemical nature of any physical substance making up external form. Mineral matter is always mineral even in a human body. Were this not so reproduction of vegetable or animal cells would be possible in the laboratory. The stalactitic growths in some chemical mixtures are far from life. Despite occasional claims science has been unable to bridge the boundaries of domain and indeed no link between any two of the kingdoms exists even from animal to closely allied man. Vegetable substance includes mineral matter. The higher kingdoms contain all the lower. Constitution in complex form does not cut off activity in subordinate domains but rather controls it.

Materialism ignores the sharp boundaries of domain. Yet the limitations are constant and obvious.

What is life? It is not chemistry for then the digestive acids in the intestinal tract of man and animal would digest the tissue of the tract as well as the content and in fact they do so immediately upon the substraction of the life principle in any case of sudden death after feeding. The kingdom boundaries are sharp, definite and immutable in the objective sphere. But they are not exclusive. Vegetable is also mineral, animal contains and embraces the other two and man is the sum of four kingdoms and therefore exists actively and truly in four domains. The occult definition of man is a conscious entity in fourfold existence. The human stage is always this focal fourth position irrespective of the outer aspect.[1]

A given form belongs to the highest domain or most complex kingdom in which its sentient life can function consciously. All substance manifests some sort of sentient life. Form of a higher domain always manifests also the sentience of all lower kingdoms active in the same great sphere of being.

THE DOMAINS OF NATURE

The objective domains of nature are four in number. They may be analyzed first by activity or the cycle of life-stream which is simple domain, secondly by substance or essential dimension which is the relative complexity of form constitution and thirdly by objective form or subdivision of being in essen-

---

[1]The pudding-bags of apt Theosophical description are correctly designated men in a preracial stage.

tial pattern which is the structure of activity in function.

Activity, substance and form are the trinity of being embodied in the golden truth.[1]

Activity is unceasing impulse, the pulsation of being, the undifferentiated cosmic force known through universal gravitation, the first emanation and last indrawing of the Great Central Flame and objectively eternal duration or time as a primary dimension. This is the Father of orthodoxy.

Substance is the indestructible constitution of being, the star dust or fundamental atoms of matter, the great deep or cosmic mother principle in nature, the first creation and last dissolution of the universe, the never-ceasing giving forth from itself of the Great Central Flame and fundamentally darkness and chaos or space as a primary dimension. This is the Holy Spirit or Paraclete in Christianity.[2]

Fruitage of activity and substance is form which grows from activity to create activity and which takes in and gives off constantly the substance of its

[1]Cf. p. 48.

[2]The common order of Father, Son and Holy Spirit is based upon Matthew, 28:19. The familiar benediction in 2 Cor., 13:14 moves the Son to first position but leaves the Holy Spirit last. The Greek fathers regarded the Spirit as the sanctity or the holy state and nature of the Father and hence correlated this usual third member to the God-power in substance. They regarded the Son as the wisdom of the Father or the insight into and obedience to divine law which in this text correlates to abstract form or God-power in pattern. Any particular order of the divine trinity is significant only in its convenience. The term Holy Ghost of the King James Bible becomes Holy Spirit in the revisions of 1885 and 1901.

material being and its objective crystallization. Form is the balance between the great cosmic attributes of time and space. It is the pattern of a being which through activity is eternal but in duration is increased or decreased in power or nature and which through substance is indestructible but in space dimension finds its point of balance either in cosmic simplicity or in complex constitution far removed from the source of all. Form is the objective reflection of being even in the most subtle or subjective of realms.

Form is life to the point of view in which inner reality is death. The inversion of form is the symbolic representation of spiritual attainment. From an understanding of this came the rite of circumcision whether concerning the prepuce or in secret the pineal gland for the spiritual operation which turns its inner surface outward and which originally was alone commanded in the development of a Jew or aspirant under the lunar mysteries.[1]   Ab-

[1]The Jew originally was an initiate or member of the chosen people who were individuals and not a racial group and were selected for hieratic purposes rather than for first Aryan colonization as sometimes supposed. (Cf. foot-note[3] p. 235.) This meaning of Jew was lost in the development of the zodiac types into the traditional twelve tribes. In the lunar mysteries clairvoyant development was demanded in advance of knowledge and this reverse of the present solar procedure made circumcision important. Lunar or solar is a convenient designation for the negative and positive methods of instruction respectively in both ancient mysteries and modern inner occultism. The lunar initiation was open only to those who were entitled to illumination from birth by interlife membership in some brotherhood. (Cf. foot-note[2] p. 200.) The last great white lodge of the lunar mysteries was the School of Samuel and its final blazing meteor was Jeremiah.

stract form or cosmic pattern never can be destroyed but may be strengthened or weakened and may be changed or modified.

Basic form is a pattern to which activity shapes substance. Form is the Son of the cosmic trinity and is Christ both as historic teacher or example to humanity and as the mundane pattern seed of the solar myth drawn into the globe as an indwelling consciousness there to be a bridge in form or understanding between cycles of the macrocosm or that world in which the planet has citizenship and the microcosm or human domain in which man's ego patterns itself in image of the greater universe. Truly without the Christ or humanity's divine matrix man would have no spiritual rebirth. Even physical form or the body itself is the Way and Life and is to be developed and spiritualized but never denied or despised.

The domains of nature taken by activity or cycle and by substance or essential dimension provide the two macrocosmic out of the three present analyses of form. These are the familiar kingdoms taken from two complementary aspects.

By cycle nature possesses four objective domains. The mineral kingdom is the material earth substance. This reveals the cycle of the planet itself. The mineral or chemical atoms remain inert on the globe throughout the cosmic days of manifestation and nights of inactivity or from that first creation of matter until that final universal dissolution which mark the full life of Brahma and the great day of a solar system.[1]

The vegetable kingdom is the earth's planetary consciousness. The principle of this kingdom ensouls egos of a life-stream superior to mineral matter and is manifest in periods of activity and of repose roughly relative to the sleeping and waking states of man.[2] The temperature, magnetic pulse, geographic circulations and moods of cataclysmic and epidemic expressions of the earth function in the channels of this kingdom's being. Earthquakes, weather and all the electrical phenomena of the globe are centered here in effect and in cause.

The animal and human kingdoms respectively are unconsciously and consciously parasitic upon the earth. These kingdoms remain upon a particular globe for a period shorter than the two subordinate life-streams by many millions of years. The animal types are created and developed solely in relation to the earth but the human form is perfected as a pattern by constant contrast with outer cosmic environment. The animal life-stream comes to the globe and leaves concurrently with the activity cycles of the vegetable kingdom but whereas in a sense the life-stream of the second domain departs and returns to the same physical globe in much the same way that the self of a man in sleep leaves and returns to the body and yet normally hovers close in

[1]A period. Cf. p. 205.
[2]The rounds. Cf. p. 208.

its absence the animal life-stream migrates from planet to planet in a larger space cycle.[1]

The human life-stream also moves from physical globe to physical globe in the divine space scheme but at shorter periods of eons of duration as roughly represented by geological or glacial periods which cut off individualization through the lack of ecliptic obliquity.[2] The physical human form as a pattern type undergoes change only in this cycle of planetary steps in the solar system and only alters in cosmic worlds above the physical.[3] Man is said to be created in the image of God to symbolize this.

By dimension nature possesses four material domains also identified through the kingdoms. The

[1]Of the three gifts of Venus to earth in occult tradition the bees and the ants were brought to the globe by the Pandean humanity while wheat could not be brought and was developed upon the planet by Venus initiates. All three were left and preserved in certain caverns by protective magic during the great cataclysms which destroyed and completely remodeled the surface of the continents. By later Atlantean magic both vegetable and animal form was changed in many cases. The vegetable forms persist as in the banana but the only wide-spread animal survival is the wasp which was developed from the bee and has been held upon the globe by the larger cycle invoked for the honey gatherer.

[2]This does not leave a globe without its necessary fourth life-stream influence. (Cf. p. 104.) The analogy is to the development of a human form in cooperation with higher principles already linked to the physical nucleus for their concurrent development in superior domain. (Cf. p. 157.) The interchange of human life-streams from planet to planet gives each globe its necessary chemical stimulation and its activity pattern. This exchange is cyclic but also is gradual and is accompanied by overlapping (cf. p. 240) and recapitulation (Cf. p. 88).

[3]Despite the staggering age of geological remains no development of human form is exhibited which yet demonstrates a greater deviation from general type than is to be found in existing human races.

names of the kingdoms not only label the form
groups which mark the domains objectively but here
indicate the fundamental types of consciousness in
complexity or at various stages of natural consistency[1] in form.

The mineral consistency is simple or one-dimen-
sional and is marked by inertness. This purely material substance has no phenomena of its own and
no quality but simple response. The chemical com-
positions which lie behind its structure are themselves induced or stimulated to their actions and reactions. A mountain chain is thrown up by cataclysm and is worn down by erosion. Fertility and
barrenness of soil are imparted qualities. When
the life principle is subtracted from any physical
form *rigor mortis* ensues and the body from which
individual being in any of the three higher kingdoms
has withdrawn lies subject to the slower chemical
action which is induced by the sentient life of the
planet and is marked in the mineral kingdom while
a function of vegetable consistency. The consciousness of mineral consistency is response. Mineral
matter remains static in form and position except
as moved or changed by the play of force and activity around and through it.

[1]Consistency as here used is not in strict accordance with dictionary authority but is employed with the addition of a definite
mathematic technical sense to the kitchen meaning of the word.
Higher form adds to lower a complexity that figuratively might be
taken as a spiritual thickening but which is also an inclusion in
each case of an extra element of consistence that is not unity either
in activity or substance.

The vegetable consistency of nature is two-dimensional and is marked by the possibility of expansion or simple growth. This is the cosmic quality of fluidity and is not a mere response of matter elements to lines and geometric figures of force but is the addition of a new domain. Fundamental space or all-dimension here divides into separative units through which the primary emanation or cosmic impulse can set up cycles of repetition. Here is the inherent vibration of all things. The distinction between mineral and vegetable is akin to that between the solid and fluid states of matter because the latter is a recapitulation within the mineral domain of the essential difference between these first two domains. In the fluid created by increase of temperature or life possibility comes a greater relative separation of atoms through the growth of mutually cooperative attraction and repulsion. This is vibration within the mass and it gives the pliability through which expansion and change may take place.

The four types of this fluidity are known to the occultist as ethers and are recognized as extracts induced between atoms in magnetic relationship. The word etheric is also applied to the double in the body and to the higher physical plane. These variant uses of the term permit a confusing assumption of identity between the four ethers and the vegetable principle or second domain.[1] The domain, the

---

[1]The term etheric must be kept in both senses because of wide

etheric double and the vegetable kingdom are created by two-dimensional manifestation in matter. The ethers actually are physical but correspond in order to the various domains in which the activity materialized and crystallized through them centers. In each kingdom the life process produces its distinctive magnetic essence.

The first or chemical[1] ether supports vibration and is within the range of human instruments. It is well represented by the allotropic form of elements such as ozone in the atmosphere or carbon in charcoal. The second or life ether as the material substance of the vegetable domain is the vehicle of simple consciousness in all sentient form and while mostly rare in constitution and beyond the range of physical measurement it is yet chemically represented by the subtle invisible potency in the narcotics, hypnotics and particularly in the catalytic hormones of higher life. These two lower ethers of occult philosophy together constitute the double of sentient form. The first essence provides the vehicle of expansion and the second the plasma for consciousness response. Subtracted together at death they are succeeded by *rigor mortis* and decay.

The higher consistencies include the first two. Both animal and man build their outer inert form

usage. No dictionary authority exists for either meaning while in conventional occult systems a great variation exists in the employment of both. Cf. *prana, linga-sarira* and etheric double in Appendix B, p. 255.

[1]These names are from conventional Rosicrucian teachings.

of mineral matter. Through vegetable constitution each of the higher kingdoms gains the bare quality of fluidity but with additional specialization so that the chemical atoms may function in the more complex higher forms. The further specialization of fluidity is identified in terms of additional ethers. The occultist understands that these are not extra quantities of subtle matter but are change in quality of substance as in the transformation from solid to liquid or from liquid to gaseous state.

The light ether is the essence in matter which permits it to be the vehicle of all transfer of heat, light or sensual intelligence. This essence is induced in the animal consistency of being. Physical animal form precedes vegetable activity upon a planet in its awakening to activity and consciousness. Only through the human and animal life-streams is heat engendered. The Bible knows precisely of what it speaks when in the more material account of creation light appears before the heavenly bodies and in the other account the self-conscious animal or man is brought into being as a necessary adjunct to rain and vegetation.[1]

[1]Being is the active principle of human manifestation and man is the limitation and yet the necessary supporting inductive agency of vegetable constitution while light in the first instance is a symbol for the duration which differentiates or divides *manvantara* or day from *pralaya* or night and therefore is the limitation and support of form or objective constitution. In the initial account of creation the first day brings forth duration as the response to the manifestation. The creative word itself is the limitation or control of this duration. Space follows as the creation of the second day or the firmament of cosmic relationship responsive to duration and limited

The reflecting ether is the condition of material matter that permits it to be the vehicle of imagery or memory and which aids conscious responsible development of being through reduplication of images or the projection of pattern into substance. This is the physical essence produced by the conscious activity of man through the human consistency of being. As the two lower ethers belong to the body these upper essences belong to the indwelling intelligence or ego and so alone cloak it in its activity outside the body but in the physical world. It is the development through higher faculties of these particular ethers that produces the golden aura of initiates or the solar wedding garment of divine incarnation within.

The third consistency in objective manifestation is the animal which is three-dimensional and is marked by the achievement of physical self-consciousness or an awareness of form and substance. Here is the possibility of movement or separativeness in being and of outer response to inner craving or conversely inner response to outer desire. Added to growth

by the divine manifestation. Form or pattern is the third creation in response to space or inherent relationship and the figure of speech is seed. In the fourth day come the planets or symbols of all being as plainly stated in the authorized text. On the fifth day objective growth follows in the picture of a swarm of flying and creeping things. The sixth day brings the creation of animal and man as here the symbol of motion or the outward signature of passion in the individual absolute. The seventh day corresponds to the inertia or simple reflex which is the sole activity of the first dimension and which constitutes the Sabbath in cosmic process. Cf. Appendix A, p. 254 and foot-note[2] p. 126

and vibration are fullness and depth of being. Gained is the ability to know satiation or hunger whether in the simple passions of the animal or the more complex emotions of reflex and induction in the human. Substance is the entire basis of the present objective world.[1] The animal consistency embodies inert matter in substance for further growth in supersensual realms.

The human consistency of nature is four-dimensional and is marked by the conquest and control of form. Here true conscious being is the climax of fourfold development in a fourfold body functioning through an objectively fourfold world.[2]

These are the four consistencies functioning in the four kingdoms. Here are the domains taken by activity or cycle and by substance or dimension.

Similarly the domains are established through objective form itself. The method is by analysis of essential pattern and by the diagram of functional activity. Man or the microcosm in full reflection of the universe is taken as the type although the same principles achieve identical results in all detailed occult biological study. But in the human form the somatic divisions correspond to the kingdoms and so mark the domains handily. Man's emotional nature or the signature of humanity in consciousness interprets these domains in correlation

[1]Substance is the consideration of the chapter following. Cf. p. 114 ff.

[2]Being is the consideration of the second chapter following. Cf. p. 144 ff.

to the divisions through human sensation. For this purpose the Revelation of John or apocalyptic physiological scheme is used.

The first domain is reflected in the sacral region[1] where lies the pattern in cabalistic tradition of the prior life both of the individual and the race. The sacral somatic division corresponds to the element earth whose gift[2] in spiritual development is sacrifice.[3] The whole of honest phallic instruction in occultism is built upon a recognition of the inherent power centered in this region. The duality of man or his position in balance of form is based upon the possibility of wastage at this end of the pole accompanied by drain of spiritual force and by diminution or complete destruction of the brain function at the top. The golden spinal vapor[4] mounts up within the osseous serpent to hold the brain in spiritual lubrication. The golden aura of the initiate is an etheric essence specialized in the tiny coccygeal gland at the base of the spine and appearing as the blaze that mounts and bathes the egg of being set in the symbolic Rosicrucian chalice.

[1]Region as here used should not be confused with the Rosicrucian substitution of the word for plane. Cf. foot-note[1] p. 127.

[2]The inborn talent or natural endowment which in a sense gives itself to that individual who discovers the power of the element within. This idea is familiar in fairy tales where the people of the elements must offer presents whether under compulsion or willingly to all who discover them.

[3]The ability to unclutch and to let go in obedience to the Rosicrucian dictum marks a spiritual independence of enmeshing *karma* and illustrates the gift of sacrifice in its receipt by an individual.

[4]An amber fluid when tapped.

The second domain is reflected in the abdominal region and is the somatic division centered at the solar plexus or general reflex center. Here is the focus of growth through all departments of being and the full source of bodily power and vitality. The region corresponds to the sea whose gift in spiritual development is faith. The lunar mysteries spoke through the abdomen and the voice of prophecy at Delphi actually articulated through the viscera of the pythoness. In the East where the individualization and personal responsibility of the solar school have never been given except to a favored few the method of development is largely centered in the postures which by actual position as in pressure of the soles of the feet against the body with regular breathing to exert diaphragmatic stimulation and by protracted visual contemplation of the navel work wholly through this lower central somatic division.

The third domain corresponds to the cardiac center and the heart or to the field of the passions and impulses of human experience. The seed-atom of the physical body is held here until initiation and in this somatic division the battles of the spirit are waged. According to the Apocalypse this is the region of rivers and springs. The gift in spiritual development is prophecy or understanding. Courage or fear, tolerance or bigotry and all basic human qualities of character are centered here.

The fourth domain is related to the throat or the pharyngeal center associated with voice and with the human attribute of vocal articulation or creative expression. In the Apocalyptic imagery this realm is the sky out of which descends the gift of tongues or the ability to interpret all things. Conscious understanding makes man a responsible citizen in his sphere. Through the throat he becomes divine and may even call life into being by the spoken word.

THE SCIENCE OF CORRELATION

Organization of the occult conceptions of form is more simple than outline of the vast superphysical sphere. In the field of objective things and of molded substance every last tiny subdivision of being is important and significant. A sense of domain is as necessary to the student as a grasp of more elementary supersensual conceptions of time and space. But the detailed study and analysis of form is the function of occult science and a work in general too large for particular tabulation. Only the method is of present interest.

The science of correlation itself is based wholly upon the golden truth of occult philosophy. Activity shows large cycles pictured in each of smaller ones that constitute them. Through comparison of cycles astrology employs divination. Substance reveals the orderly constitution of all things in greater spheres which include subordinate ones created in reflection of the larger pattern. From this spherical relationship comes divination by numerology and by symbols as in psychism. Form itself in its pattern and in the cyclic subdivision of all its parts correlates to all other factors.

A man's palm, his head, his foot, the iris of his eye and the relative shape and position of parts of his body all give accurate clue to matters of his past or future. Business employment officers study noses and hands. Theatrical producers examine ankles. Psychics read human auras while psychoanalysts translate dreams. Results are often amazing and yet these pseudosciences are empiric and only indicate the truth which because it lies deep interests the occultist.

In supersensual philosophy the relationship between all things is determined by a simple interplay of two complementary processes which show the duality or essential polarity of primary constitution. These work through the domain of being and are studied in the balance which is form.

The first process is specialization or the adaptation of grosser activity, substance and form to the use of higher. This is general increase in the consistency of being and spiritually it is crystallization. It marks the conquest of simpler kingdoms by more complex. In the somatic divisions of sentient life it is the emphasis of the lower by a deeper plunge into limitation of general function for the achievement of greater skill, knowledge and experience in the narrower sphere.

Specialization of mineral matter is shown by sentient life in the bones, skin, nails and particular organic, nerve and glandular structure as well as in elementary sense tissues and simple plasma common to plant and to higher form. The cellular activity of the tissues and fluids in man and animal displays specialization of vegetable principle in this highest objective constitution. Man further particularizes animal nature in the emotional function of the human blood.

The second process is universalization or the growth of lower form while used by higher and is in reflection of the more subtle principle. It is shown in all objective evolution and improvement of form type and in transitory phenomena as the acquisition of commonly human traits by domestic animals.

The science of correlation is the tracing of relationships both through simple activity and substance in the domains of nature and through function or crystallization in pattern and form types by general comparison and by analysis of the cooperative subdivisions of particular form. For this purpose the keys to knowledge are used.[1]

CONCURRENCY IN CORRESPONDENCE

Form is balance. For everything that has being a natural opposite must exist. The church has discovered this in its revivals. A man's capability for good is measured by his capacity for evil. Eternity stretches just as far backward as it does for-

---

[1] Outlined in the third chapter following, p. 181 ff. Cf. Appendix C, p. 256.

ward. The aspirant who never reverts into his yesterday will find no light in his tomorrow.

Duration and time or abstract no-dimension continue to embrace all space phenomena that evolve and spring out of first cause. The monad or constant creation and reconstitution of substance similarly embraces in its unity all form brought forth in the first trinity of being and it includes in its subdivisions all further evolution of manifestation. The balance of form exists in first cause or non-being and also in the unity of first identity. This is concurrency. Only for purposes of understanding are the processes of the universe stretched out along fine spun threads of investigation and from that necessity considered in their separateness.[1] All processes continue simultaneously and in eternal cooperation.

In the approach to correspondences in this treatise two duads have so far been introduced. Throughout the unity of space concept a distinction between objective and subjective realms is used while in the balance or duality of process revealed through form the twin cooperative factors of specialization and universalization are employed. And as that which exists objectively also has subjective being so every form specializing itself is at the same time undergoing universalization.

---

[1]Conflicts in the teachings of various occult schools and particularly among organized groups are brought about by differences in approach to life problems and by variance in method of drawing cosmic phenomena apart for analysis. Cf. p. 57.

The domains are four but it is noticeable that in activity and form they are in reality duads divided into further duality. Mineral and vegetable consistencies are actually a part of the earth while animal and man are only cooperatively so. The four ethers persistently divide into two groups and in the body commonly so separate. In the microcosm itself is found the diaphragm or a broad sheet of muscle to divide the four somatic regions into pairs. This persistent duality permits the eternal balance or concurrency in all phenomena.

Matter may be defined as crystallized vibration or as force balanced in form. Polarity or opposition is the first differentiation of creation into function. This is vibration or the essence of growth. Anything is first understood when its pole or complement is discovered. Adam in the garden of Eden possessed no true consciousness until Eve was created out of that rib which was his spine or the symbol of his establishment in balance or form.

THE DUAD AND ITS SCHOOL

The third number is the principle of dual or basically active relationship and is the Pythagorean two or duad. It is the dividing element in nature which permits simple being and is vibration, change, reflection, balance, alternation of point of view and the first personal interrelationship of being for which purpose form is created and exists.

The third school is the Cabalistic or the philo-

sophical and alchemical resolution of all things back
to first cause by correspondence. Its great teaching
is the microcosm and macrocosm or the man below
who is the reflection of the divine above. Its modern prophet is Paracelsus[1] who was the father of
homeopathy and author of the microcosmic doctrine.
Through the homeopathic school of medicine his
work has been ingrained in the consciousness of all
people. His philosophy is presumed to be dead yet
to-day man has learned the fundamental relativity
of opposites or poles in which like deals with like
and in which the very cause of a disease is its cure
through the duad applied to usefulness.

[1]Theophrastus Bombastus von Hohenheim.

CHAPTER IV

THE DOMAINS OF CONSCIOUSNESS

CONSCIOUSNESS IS SUBSTANCE

THE fourth key truth is important because it is locative. It involves a first operation in building a structure of understanding upon the initial cosmic trinity of emanation. To the universal triad of an unceasing reality in time, space and abstract form will now be added the full pentad or fivefold constitution of material being in expression.[1] The three itself or triad in the Pythagorean numeral philosophy is activity of process which can only be interpreted objectively as degree of self-awareness. Consciousness is the subjective urge behind material form or matter and is the particular expression of the mundane triad.

The use of a total of eight numbers rather than seven, nine or ten is confusing to the numerology student but consistent with the basis point of view in the present analysis. The first trinity of cosmogony involves the numbers one to three. The seven rays of the Pythagorean philosophy from the

---

[1] Thus that which is actual and tangible in direct human experience is the particular fivefold concern of this chapter with the four following.

monad to the heptad are considered in mundane matters alone.[1] Superficially these two series add to make the decad or sacred ten.

Unfortunately for all who would establish numerology as a parlor game the first three numbers or dimensions of the cosmic progression do not correspond with the terrestial series.

Upon reflection this becomes an obvious fact. The step up from a mundane to a correlated universal realm requires the addition of one dimension and the step down demands a similar subtraction. The three-dimensional world of sense is only two-dimensional in the solar sphere. The plane movements of planets and quadrant points in the celestial saucer of the zodiac are employed by astrology for direct correspondence to events in terrestrial life. An individual who wishes to attain universal consciousness in this three-dimensional manifestation must achieve a four-dimensional understanding. Because the sentient principle of life is the cosmic ensoulment of a terrestrial domain the self-awareness or consciousness which is the principle of ensoulment is dimensionally always identified as one number above the digit that classifies the outer being.[2]

This consciousness although identified dimensionally is not a quality or dimension but is a substance taking its own form in its higher being or subtle do-

[1] The conventional and familiar sevenfold schemes summarized in the eighth chapter. Cf. p. 217 ff.
[2] Cf. p. 81.

main and there it is subject to all the natural laws operative in denser mass.

Human consciousness is the four which becomes the number of its dimension in full cosmic activity and which corresponds to abstract being and to the tetrad.[1] Yet human form in its full response to objective evolution is only animal and so is objectively active as the triad.[2] Animal consciousness is the three or simple growth in separate-awareness while the animal form which is the type of both human and third-kingdom physical expression is vegetable and the duad. The vegetables in sentient principle are the two or mass consciousness in motion and the minerals the one or reflexive unity of inertia although in physical constitution the plants are the monad or simple visible emanation of form and the earth substance itself the inert reabsorbing cipher. This is analysis by a law of greatest importance in the *Codex Occultus*.[3] State of awareness is always dimensionally one power above stage of constitution.

In mundane existence where knowledge is measured by tangible chemistry or actual material structure little is to be gained by a point of view set hypothetically in heaven worlds.[4] The present perspective is from life and objective form because any properly

[1] The consideration of the chapter following. Cf. p. 144 ff.

[2] The response identifies the higher principle active in the lower constitution. Cf. Appendix A, p. 254.

[3] The law of aberration in the sphere group of the musical key under the triad.

[4] It is yet a method so commonly employed that much detail in

grounded aspirant must first know and understand sensual phenomena.[1]

For the identification of the emanative seven rays in terrestrial dimension the trinity of the cosmos is equated by subtraction of one from each of its terms. Therefore the Father has been given as the Pythagorean cipher or oudad, the Paraclete as the one or monad and the Word or Son as that duad or polarity of cooperation between upper and lower realms which accounts for the necessity of the Christ sacrifice in orthodox salvation.

The numbers of terrestrial consideration are eight. The octad or eight itself and ennead or nine are active only in recapitulative processes beyond the scope of introductory principles but yet are important and an integral part of the *Codex Occultus*. The cosmic four or tetrad which corresponds to the lower triad itself passes normal human comprehension because it is fifth-dimensional in the earth sphere. Similarly the other higher cosmic numbers are of no interest except in initiation.

Consciousness is substance because it is the literal constitution of being through space dimension. Superficially consciousness is the self-awareness of being in terrestrial activity.

The fourth key truth is particularly useful because

this treatise will seem wholly at variance with earlier but here recognized as authoritative modern teachings of occult philosophy.

[1]That seeker who does not keep within the center of his sphere faces an intellectual confusion frequently noticeable in the popular fields of occult philosophy. Cf. p. 125.

it serves to locate the focus of intelligent control through all phenomena and to guide the investigator toward proper identifications in any active field of fundamental coordinates. The sentient stimulation of being is structurally different in man, animal, plant and inert matter. This difference is relative and is a matter of dimension made most clear through numeral philosophy.

Consciousness is not itself dimension but is the substance of any superior domain through which self-awareness of lower being may be focused. Mineral consciousness is the sustaining etheric principle of objective sentient constitution, plant consciousness or the extract from this vital principle of all higher life is the astral substance in which the animal self-awareness of beast and man clothes itself and animal consciousness or awareness of desire is the higher astral or mental stuff in which human emotional expression is crystallized. Thus the Rosicrucian whose school is interested in the process of things speaks of vital and desire bodies while the Theosophist trained in understanding of the constitution of life names these inner principles of the human organism the etheric double and astral body respectively.

No orderly scheme of supersensual life remains for scientific analysis if consciousness is confused with the qualities and dimensions of being or is taken as a vague and intangible attribute of sentient activity rather than as an evolutionary result of expression. But little perplexity is possible if consciousness when traced to its realm of being is recognized as normal substance reacting to ordinary natural law. The conception of worlds in occult philosophy permits this orderly study and is the great contribution of the triad and tetrad occult schools[1] to modern metaphysical thought. Foundation of this conception is the fourth key truth which becomes the most valuable of the series.

THE OCCULT CONCEPTION OF WORLDS

The trained student of any degree in occult philosophy is quite at home with the worlds and planes of being. Here is the kindergarten of supersensual investigation. Whether visualized as heaven with or without a hell added and whether dealing with the normal and its subconscious or merely with life and its borderland the metaphysican is more than at ease over or through the veil.[2]

The astral realm is the playground and the proving ground of the occultist. There he performs healing work at night and there he meets his fellows for instruction in classes or sallies forth to greet friends in and out of the body.[3] By common account the living and the dead intermingle freely. Poetry, novels, philosophies and apocalyptic productions are dictated from the unseen. The modern bookstores are well stacked with accounts both broadly

[1]The Rosicrucian and Theosophical groups respectively. Cf. pp. 140, 165.
[2]A term without dictionary authority but current in occult philosophy for the sensual boundary of the physical realm.
[3]Cf. clairvoyance and imagination, p. 20.

general and greatly in detail of this life after death supposed to be shared in such manner by the living.

Did an appreciable degree of agreement exist in the bulking literature upon this subject the way of the seeker would be less difficult. Yet the very number of irreconcilable descriptions and the fact itself of extreme divergence in eye-witness narratives yield the simple explanation of the matter and at the same time lend additional proof to the hypothesis of occult philosophy.

An account gains nothing from its first-hand source. The psychological tests in colleges have demonstrated an extreme unreliability in average observation. Evidence gains or loses value only in the degree of competency revealed by the witness. A child is unfitted to obtain and to transmit accurate impressions of any but the simplest phenomena in an adult material world. The voyager in supersensual realms is even less competent than the physical infant because he faces an increased complexity of being due to the added cosmic dimension in astral phenomena. The value of first-hand information is through popular appeal alone. The scientist discounts sensual accuracy in any realm.

Experience in supersensual worlds is by necessity the result of an extension or enlargement of consciousness. Awareness of any sort is a function of consciousness. Consciousness is substance or the embodiment of experience through awareness in the emotion or thought stuff of higher realm.

The only difference between a dream and objective reality is the matter of duration. Commonly the events of material life are sharper in sensual record but not necessarily. Lowly evolved humans go through a waking dream in life and only in nightmares approach real sensation. Imagination is the process of development in consciousness. Sharpness of reality gains proportionately with imaginative growth. In hallucination or dreams and even in simple mental processes the actual literal instinctive drawing of subtle substance about the mental image in order to clothe it in being may be seen clearly by a skilled clairvoyant. The fact that materialization in a spiritualistic seance may be faintly ethereal or seemingly solid and actual to the point of delicate and firm life-throbbing flesh depends upon the relative strength of the will to materialize and upon the cooperating wills in the circle and this is no more than a physical illustration of the phenomenon common in higher realms. A man creates and constantly remodels his own astral world and so therein meets events or persons as the caprice of his mood dictates.

Such an understanding of occult philosophy is far from the materialistic view of a supersensual realm constituted in pure delusion. Here are conditions which result rather from the extreme fluidity of upper space in contrast to lower and more crystallized being. While in spiritualistic circles the discarnate forms drawn to the sitter are generally recreated by him from his own specialized etheric substance and

so are given expressive faculty through vital emana-
tions from his body or that of the medium yet these
forms whether drawn to convey intelligence or to
materialize are first recreated in substance on patterns or type shells which exist and have some affinity
for him.[1]

The astral world from any higher perspective possesses infinitely more reality than the physical realm
of present being. Through its fifth-dimensional nature it not only cradles individual evolution in underlying processes which incarnate and stabilize consciousness in form but it provides the realm of fluidic
action and reaction of thought or emotion by which
the imagination has full play. Through the latter
activity human consciousness is developed into further evolution. This composite nature of the astral
and of all higher realms of space is analyzed in the
evolutionary schemes of being.[2] The understanding here of importance is that all voyages into supersensual awareness whether in imagination, dreams or
conscious clairvoyance are determined and influenced
entirely by the physical circumstances of the voyager.
His investigations do not reveal supra-actualities but
only superattenuations of his own experience.[3]

[1]Occult investigation through many modern groups has shown
that at definite evolutionary or development stages the central intelligence or ego of the human being may be found upon the astral
plane and that the phenomenon of earth-bound spirits is possible
particularly in the case of suicide or those accidental deaths where
the body of man is destroyed but the life tie of higher principles is
left unsevered.

[2]The consideration of the seventh chapter. Cf. p. 192 ff.

[3]Of this the conventional heavens are a fine psychological dem-

What then is the nature and constitution of super-organic realms? The question literally is unanswerable. In practice it is akin to a description of love to one who has never known passion or of spiritual ecstasy to the man who has yet to know true religion.

In effect it is explaining to the mineral atom which dwells in the physical plane those things that indicate the feeble consciousness of the plant which has gained a cosmic consistency through the etheric plane. The plant swells to greet the sun or retards the flow of its sap to meet cold, storm and darkness. The plant knows the joy of spring and of growth and it senses the gentle calm of summer in which it can display gratitude for its being through its flower and perfume. With autumn it puts its soul and hope into its seed and it cheerfully yields the pods to the scattering wind of coming winter or else perhaps it gives fruit to animal or man who in enjoyment of eating spreads the seeds abroad. Through all this the mineral atom remains the same. It rests inert and content to be placed where the forces leave it in one or another chemical composition.

Yet to the atom it can be demonstrated that this association with others of its kind leads to the plant's specialization of all of them into a higher and more complex form. The atom by lesser experience in its own being and tiny realm will discover a subtle

onstration. The other world was a happy hunting-ground to the American Indian, a divine fatigueless brothel to the oriental sensualist and is now a cosmic ice-box to the blue-law bigot.

change and will grow into knowledge of results in pattern of its greater usefulness in that plane where it has yet no consciousness.

Similarly to man the reality of higher worlds can be explained by analogy through his normal experience.

Any reality in a superior realm of being is indicated in a lower sphere by cooperative or conscious association of units. In the case of man this is the explanation of the occult brotherhoods and of the objective humanitarian movements which reflect the world's growing universal consciousness. In first steps of growth downward from the larger spheres to this physical proving-ground mankind was established in great races of blood or immutable association so that he could be controlled from above and could thus be guided through the infancy of his evolution. In the final stages of his development he will consciously again draw into a globewide race unity of tolerant cooperation which when voluntarily and willingly assumed by each member is the true brotherhood of man.

On higher planes the divine guides of humanity known as the creative hierarchies are gathered in great brotherhoods like the earth's White Lodge. This is not because these initiates as individuals are superior to lesser men or have organized themselves to syndicate wisdom and power but because their very conscious being in supradimension demands this association. Unassociated they could not continue to exist. Each would immediately relapse into the unconsciousness or loss of identity suffered by normal man between lives.[1]

Supersensual experience must always be gained through the matrix of physical being. Each man is the center of his sphere and must build his own path of initiation as well as his vehicles of expression out of this center. If his sphere is small his produced phenomena in higher realm whether imagination, dreams or clairvoyance will be transitory and illusionary. He can only achieve the durable reality above or the eternity of orthodoxy by growing into association with other human beings so that in cooperation all may be specialized in manner exactly akin to mineral atoms used in higher forms. Spiritually and actually here is the invisible church and the true body of Christ.

Supersensual consciousness is marked in the physical world by sentient growth in the individual's life or being and by change in his point of view or expression. The investigator well applies pragmatic tests to any glittering glimpses of astral light. If he gains that greater sense of service which is an emerging into a larger sphere through unbegrudging

[1]Here is an explanation of the necessity for a terrestrial temple whether visibly active or not. For similar reasons a certain number of the brothers in the symbolical proportion of five out of twelve must remain in the temple not as a literal dwelling therein but as an expression of focal interest away from those earth affairs which might dissipate the force of the lodge. This group-consciousness of the brotherhood is fixed in higher realms solely to maintain a spiritual reservoir which through them is linked with lower life and made available for all uninitiated men.

gradual surrender of self which is the little sphere then he may know he has approximated reality. But if he despises the self in hope of greater being he has only surrendered his center and so has lost his bearings and his usefulness. A love of humanity and a wish for universal brotherhood or a cultivation of sympathy and a growth of interest in any cosmic process marked by the purposes of the White Lodge through politics, economics or social movements all indicate that the seeker is evolving through higher planes into a greater eternal reality. Yet this is so only if these things come out of his cultivation of experience in minor matters. In petty affairs is first marked the specialization which takes place within him who discovers himself an atom in a larger world.[1]

The consistencies of nature reveal the multiple constitution of matter from the focus of higher intelligence turned in upon its constituting elements. The reversed point of view into enlarged sphere from smaller situation gives the occult conception of worlds.[2]

[1]Intellectualism empty in vanity or self-exaltation marks not a punishable violation of divine ethics but rather a focus of consciousness in the small sphere of personality which therefore is clue to a false and ephemeral illumination to be enlarged rather than condemned or destroyed.

[2]This chapter therefore in the process of turning from the cosmic to the terrestrial inverts the point of view of its predecessor. Cf. foot-note[1] p. 114 which cites a prior inversion in a larger sphere of consideration. The principle of cosmic reversal in the *Codex Occultus* is the law of divergence in the correspondence group of the phallic key under the hexad.

In these perspectives of being the key to subordinates is form and the guide to superiors is consciousness.

THE DOMAINS OF CONSCIOUSNESS

In occult philosophy a technical distinction must be made between the terms world and plane.[1] A world defines any universal sphere of being in its boundary of consciousness. A plane is a world division created by a differentiation of substance in activity.

Occult tradition gives a total of seven worlds but three of these are beyond anything but the theoretical or hypothetical ken of the investigator and so are here ignored. Each world is further divided into seven conditions by the states of its matter[2] but even in the physical world only four of these states are known to science and are the solid, liquid, gaseous and fourth state of Crookes. Subjectively all space is built upon the seven or number of manifestation. Yet in objective existence and normal cognition the four of crystallization or the quadrants of being must be taken as the basis of understanding.

The usual division of all fourfold schemes into duads is found again in the great consciousness domains since these worlds naturally fall into twin

[1] The extension of the term world to identify complete similar but supersensual realms is common in metaphysical writings and yet possesses no dictionary authority. The specific use of world and of the accepted term plane in this treatise is arbitrary but in close conformity with general occult usage although region is substituted for plane by many Rosicrucian schools. Cf. foot-note[3] p. 208.

[2] Summarized in the seventh chapter. Cf. p. 212 ff.

groups.   One lower duad wholly embraces normal objective expression.[1]   The higher produces that outward abnormality[2] which in the present state of man's evolution is the signature of a truly human or separative activity.   And in the great consciousness scheme an additional factor of importance results from the division of each world into two planes for a polarization of particular world activity.   These three cooperate and active duads identify and so introduce the triad or terrestrial three of functioning life.[3]

[1]For the worlds and planes cf. Appendix B, p. 255 and note the sharp division above the astral in the schemes given by all schools. Despite the confusion in various identifications the realms above the astral are clearly marked in their separate general nature.

[2]Precocity, soul development or initiation and at the lower reflective pole brilliant perversities and insanity.

[3]The next step in dimensional evolution above the two is the three and this obviously cannot be merely the addition of a third consideration into an existing two but rather must be the creation of an entirely new factor by a cooperate change which takes place in the primary two and is therefore expressed solely in such a third. The planes are this expression of the triad and yet they are themselves dual and are only analyzed by the duad. (Cf. foot-note p. 162.)   The dimensional association of two related duads creates the inverse reflection of each in the other and leads to the division of each member of each duad into two. (Mathematically this is the multiplication by two of the product through addition of two and two or is an eight in the Pythagorean world schemes.   By celestial mathematics simple addition expands a consideration in any dimension but multiplication is the compound addition necessary for the achievement of a dimensional enlargement of any consideration. The duad alone may be added to itself or multiplied once by itself to produce an identical result and therefore the duad is the natural foundation for mathematical evolution.)   The physical world reflects the spiritual world and the astral the mental.   The physical plane reflects the lunar plane.   The etheric reflects the astral and this results in the wide confusion between these two.   Here respectively are the activities of simple duads in two different dimen-

The first world is the physical.[1] This is the objective universe or is matter as an inert whole. It includes the earth and all material phenomena upon it. It embraces the other planets and members of the solar system together with the visible heavens and every active star or darkened wanderer of space. Only through this world is higher understanding obtained or consciousness induced. It divides into two planes or the physical and etheric.

The physical plane or chemical region[2] is the static physical world and it consists of matter in the

sions of consciousness as worlds and planes or in terrestrial and individual fields respectively. But the physical plane also reflects the fire plane, the etheric the spirit, the astral the solar and the lunar the mental. This interduad activity in the superior scheme is the triad and becomes that process of soul extraction from vehicle substance which underlies conventional Rosicrucian teachings. It is an abstruse demonstration to a mind that has not first mastered the duad understanding which is an initial consideration throughout this treatise. More difficult yet to the casual seeker is the dimensional comprehension of the tetrad which except in explanation of one particular detail of wide-spread disagreement lies beyond any useful employment in practical life. To produce this dimensional tetrad the duad again is multiplied by itself and so raised to its fourth power or to sixteen which becomes the heptad by arithmetical or occult resolution to the digit that in numeral philosophy identifies it in any objective sphere. This seven is therefore the number of manifestation throughout a tripolarized universe of fourfold being. In the scheme of worlds the additional dimension is represented by an association of the lunar and mental planes not only by inverse reflection but also by a juxtaposition which transforms this added dimensional relationship into a unity from inferior perspective so that apparently they merge and create fourth position in any sevenfold scheme of states. This merging has led to the persistent objective identification of worlds in the sevenfold scheme by which the sphere of the complete tetrad is split into stages. Cf. Appendix B, p. 255.

[1]Cf. Appendix B, p. 255.
[2]The Rosicrucian term. Cf. foot-note[1] p. 106.

seven states of objective constitution.[1]   No distinction will make clear to the materialist the difference between this plane and the world which contains it. It represents and stands for the first world.

The etheric plane or alchemic region is the dynamic field of the physical world.   This plane contains the ethers or essences obtained by preternatural processes of life in the various occult consistencies.[2] It differentiates the activities of material substance. No physical phenomena take place without etheric support.

The astral world[3] is the subjective realm that supports all visible and known life.   It is the fluid cosmic sensitiveness in which objective being throbs in growth or decay.   It is the great subconscious or the land just through the veil.   It divides into two planes or the astral and lunar.

The astral plane is the static astral world or the substance of emotion and thought which is acted upon by imagination, will, desire and the superphysical intrusion of conscious discarnate or living entities.   It is the normal heaven region and also inconsiderately is hell and purgatory. Here individual expression disrupts itself.   Tendencies and form are influenced towards a return to type. Upon this plane are the sustaining shells of settled habits, prejudices

[1]For the seven states cf. p. 212.
[2]Outlined in the third chapter.   Cf. p. 101 ff. and foot-note p. 210.
[3]Cf. p. 119.

and inclinations. Obsessions and bodily or moral degeneracies with all ingrained abnormalities are here established in being. This substance supplies form to the animal nature of man.

The lunar plane or soul region is the dynamic astral world where is fought the Armageddon or constant spiritual battle of the human spark. This is the plane of essences drawn from astral experience. The emotional envelopes of all being are tested and refined in consciousness developed in this fourth realm of man's being. Ordinarily and normally human self-awareness is focused upon this plane. The functions of concrete thought[1] or discursive reason take place by comparison of images materialized in higher astral essence. Here humanity above the adolescent stage actually lives and has its being. Only that lucid, fluid and dispassionate mentality found in some few scattered individuals is able to carry consciousness above this plane.

The physical and astral worlds define all normal manifestation of objective sentient life and are the lower duad of planetary expression. In the physical universe matter is limited to its place of being and in the physical great world no contact is possible between the earth globe and other heavenly bodies except in meteoric exchange. The astral world as a superior invisible cosmos containing the physical universe is the lunar ocean. Through astral phenomena intercourse exists between any planet and its

[1] Cf. foot-note[6] Appendix B, p. 255.

moons[1] but no possible individually conscious transcendence of the planet's own great sphere[2] can take place.

The mental[3] world is the third great domain of consciousness. This is unknown and untouched by the vast mass of humanity. Only individuals who truly reincarnate[4] and who have an actual *karma* in consciousness from life to life may develop awareness within this world. The reborn personality which carries a non-conscious *karma* akin to the type tendencies of a plant or of a species functions through the astral world and lunar ocean. The mental world is the field of the initiate or the elder brother of man who must possess self-awareness through solar consciousness. As a world it lies before and beyond any sense of separateness in humanity yet it is touched slightly in material altruism and in those fine arts or creative handiwork in form which intuitionally express life and character. It divides into two planes or the mental and solar.

The mental plane is the static region of the world. Here the egos of man are seed-atoms or sparks of divine substance. In this plane is centered prescience

[1]Cf. foot-note p. 223.

[2]Man's sphere of activity is marked objectively in the physical while that of a planet which is an ego in the immediately higher dimension is actively focused in the astral or next superior great world.

[3]As much a misnomer as astral but equally established in usage. Cf. foot-notes pp. 16, 155[1].

[4]Those who develop a personality with active being focused above the lower duad and who therefore are not compelled to create a new personality for each life.

or that simple knowing of which intuition is a shadow. The abstract patterns or cosmic and eternal form types of all physical constitution are located here.

The solar plane is the dynamic region of the mental world where essences are drawn from divination or exercise of prescience and where all highly exalted spiritual aspiration contributes to the consciousness necessary for functioning in the initiate vehicle so created from substance of the mental plane.

The mental world lies in the cosmic ocean and it permits intercourse between the various planets and the sun. The regular cyclic movements of the initiate workers from planet to planet to stimulate and adjust evolution of racial man have given rise to an occult tradition by which the planets as bodies of the guiding planetary spirits or hierarchies are thrown off from the sun when the humanities of these bodies needed the development brought about by definite cosmic position in the solar system.[1] The astrology of process in the human living temple of the divine spirit is built entirely upon the relative position of the planetary orbits out from the sun.[2]

The spirit world or fourth of the series in occult philosophy is the cosmic fire and it is superior to any ocean or cosmic chaos of creation. It also is a

[1]At the present time (1924) a large colonization of Venus initiates is active upon the earth. Cf. p. 98, also foot-note[1] p. 242. At less frequent intervals colonizations of wholes and parts of humanities are made from globe to globe. Cf. p. 239 ff.

[2]Chaldean order. Cf. p. 222 ff., also Appendix D, p. 257.

duad. Through this fire comes intercourse between all activity or being in lower and higher supersensual worlds. The spirit plane is the region of pure spiritual substance. Of this stuff is the vehicle of a hierarch or creative god such as Jehovah constituted. The fire plane is the subtle region of essence of spirit which marks pure divine consciousness. This fourth world with the lower mental forms the upper great duad through which man escapes from the wheel of life that holds him.

These domains of consciousness constitute the active field of all process in occult philosophy and they give the first essential hypothesis for any consideration of broad terrestrial expression. Before the life-stream thread is carried through these worlds by the investigator he must analyze process itself and then consider the life dimensions of being and expression in detail.[1]

THE DUAD OF PROCESS

Process is the guide to an understanding of substance through the fundamental constitution of mass in space dimension and being. Process is therefore the key to consciousness because consciousness is substance.

Through process all sentient awareness is specialized and all non-conscious substance of lower realms in any world adapted to form and function. Even the eventual breakdown in all organism of special purpose results from some process which is subser-

[1]Therefore the present arrangement of chapters and sections.

vient to the same laws and principles as is its constructive opposite. Objective crystallization reveals and expresses activity but process itself becomes the fundamental guide to the construction and destruction or the maintenance and readaptation of outer form and so is the key both to constituent matter and to the higher substance or consciousness.

Abstract form is the matrix of all objective activity. From the opposite pole in point of view abstract activity may be directed analytically towards the crystallized form.

Perspective and point of view are essentially dual and consist of a comparison of anything with any other one thing. This comparison may be direct by employment of standards and models or may be relative by use of views or considerations taken from different focal points. The former method is sensual and objective while the other is analytical and subjective.

Relative comparison by this latter spiritual trigonometry is the procedure of the occult scientist. Direct comparison is a contributing factor to illusions of the objective and becomes useful as a symbol or illustration but is valueless unless checked by fundamental principles. Instead the active duad of relative comparison has been used in this treatise to analyze duration by domain and cycle,[1] space dimension by objectivity and subjectivity[2] and form by

[1] Cf. the first chapter, p. 37 ff.
[2] Cf. the second chapter, p. 61 ff.

specialization and universalization.[1]   Consciousness
to be understood must be subjected to analysis by
the duad of abstract process or stratification and
deviation.

This occult conception of process is illumined by
the story of the half-wit boy who hammered his head
against a brick wall and refused to listen to remon-
strance until a sympathetic onlooker coaxed the explanation from him: "It feels so good when I
stop!" This is the negative or reactive ecstasy of
cessation which marks flagellation and certain forms
of human perversion. In many departments of life
consciousness will instinctively stress the opposite
pole of its unsatiated desire. The boy pounded his
skull for lack of some other self-satisfying outgiving
of self. Frequently reformers will seek to prevent
in others that which they cannot stop or else dare
not admit within themselves. Through the duad
within the body this may become persistent masturbation in neurotic children and even in adults.[2]

Regular cycles of desire and satiation mark normal life. All abnormality is the result of interruption in this regularity of consciousness or habit expression. Irregularity, idiosyncrasy, abnormality
and eccentricity are all vital in growth and human experience both as stimulating and depressing agents.
Only when digression from normal is acute or greatly

[1] Cf. the third chapter, p. 87 ff.
[2] Recognition of the reflex of suppression whether external or internal is the whole basis of Freud in occult philosophy.

overbalanced is it in anywise unhealthy. Over-emphasized sameness is stagnation.

By stratification the cyclic regularity of process is analyzed. With cessation or retardation of local activity the substance or its phenomenon in any domain tends to settle or crystallize into set form. Thus at death the body of man or animal hardens in *rigor mortis* and sometimes holds the posture and much of the last expression of consciousness until putrefaction begins. If death has been caused by cataclysm or some tissue-protecting and overwhelming condition the form may even be petrified. Forces of decay which were tendencies present but overshadowed by the focus of being in larger domain immediately start their work.[1] But this is activity in a different sphere immeasurably slow by contrast and for analysis is to be taken separately.

By deviation the processes active in the improvement or volitional degeneration of the vehicles are revealed and analyzed. Irregularity brought about by resumption or acceleration of activity results in an overspecialization of the form or of the cycle of process and so through change or movement gives the necessary clue.

In the consideration of consciousness and of sen-

[1]The rigidity is extremely variable and marks only the definite transition from individual life activity to the planetary activity indicated by putrefaction. It starts in the muscles of the face or neck and moves downward. It gives way to decomposition in the same order so that while the upper parts may be flaccid the legs may be found rigid. The phenomenon provides a definite example of overlapping cyclic activities.

tient being action and expression are most important but only in comparison with habit and tendencies. Together these constitute the duad of process.

TRANSUBSTANTIATION IN OCCULT DOCTRINE

The eucharist is the sacrament of consciousness. Among the Essenes the simple supper outwardly was the type of a necessary cooperative association or brotherhood in supersensual realms and inwardly through metabolism was the type of assimilation into divine nature of the lower substance of man. As a sacrament it was the external sign of expansion in consciousness. Throughout orthodox churches the rite has lost significance and has become the symbol of a little-understood Christ atonement.

The eucharist in occult philosophy is not a celebration or dramatization of a historical event but is an actual intermingling of human and divine natures. The difference is only a matter of degree between the Christ sacrifice upon the cross when occured a blending of essence from the fire plane with the general fourth or reflecting earth ether and the ordinary eucharist during which substance of the solar plane is drawn within consciousness of the particular third or light ether specialized by the individual taking the host.

The greater eucharist upon Calvary opened the gate of the mysteries to those not yet conscious in the mental world. It marked the acquisition of a new occult consistency by the planet itself. In the exercise of this new degree of consciousness the in-dwelling spirit of the planet must lift up and embody in an invisible association or cosmic essence all human soul-atoms whose aspiration brings them into first touch with the process. This is the drawing up with him promised by Christ to all who follow his teachings. Here is active membership in the invisible church.

The minor eucharist prepares the way for the greater salvation through stimulation of the first of the two higher spiritual natures or soul bodies of man. Consubstantiation or the doctrine of union in substance of the communion elements with the blood and flesh of Christ is not the occult doctrine. It presupposes an equality in substance of upper and lower worlds. Any substance is essentially and wholly a part of the being in the highest conscious domain to which its lower constitution can only be contributory. In transubstantiation the whole sub-stance of the bread and wine is converted while the species or appearance alone remains unchanged.

Initiation or spiritual development leaves the outer life and aspect of man substantially the same but his consciousness is exalted in divinity. The body of Jesus was lost in cosmic identity when it be-came the substance of the Christ but in the domain of lower consciousness or the material world the mind, voice and will of Jesus directed and inter-preted the message incarnate but without terrestrial identity within him and therefore the personality of

Jesus alone spoke and made friends and enemies for the Christ spirit in Palestine.[1]

THE TRIAD AND ITS SCHOOL

Process or activity in essential nature is the three. Terrestrially it is symbolized by the triangle pointing upwards which interlaced with the downpointed cosmic triangle becomes Solomon's seal and possesses vast occult power. This cooperation of heavenly and earthly realms is that duad found throughout all basic relationship. But the duad is the relationship alone. From the two of any cooperation comes a new monad or the result.[2]

Domain and cycle permit duration to have expression in being. Objectivity and subjectivity in the basic qualities of space produce that dimensional relationship which is active matter. Specialization and universalization give birth to form as child of the balance they represent. Stratification and deviation represent the intervention of higher influence through the reaction of lower reflective being and so create the interlaced triangles of activity analyzed in consciousness and substance.

The three is the principle of being, activity, focus and essence. This is the fourth number or the Pythagorean triad. It is the expanding principle in na-

[1] The separation of the cosmic spirit under the Christ name for identity as a higher personality conscious in a terrestrial sphere through the body of Jesus regarded as the human man is both foolishly literal and very inexact. Jesus Christ never exhibited a pathological dual personality.

[2] Cf. foot-note[3] p. 128.

ture that enlarges being through the production of result from the more simple cooperations of the duads.

The fourth school is the Rosicrucian which studies nature by the activities of life and which explains spirituality by the processes and methods of self-purification. Its great teaching is the soul body or developed substantial consciousness of an initiate. The prophet is Max Heindel[1] who gave to the public the simple exposition of the Rosicrucian evolutionary scheme of occult philosophy and the ethical astrological instruction which together bear his name and who under guidance of high authority established a necessary focus of mystery teaching and a visible healing temple in the fullness of the Ezekiel cycle[2] which in this epoch controls the solar mysteries.

[1]Of the eight selections this alone enters upon real controversial ground. (Cf. foot-note p. 60.) That no one figure has left a great outward impress upon modern life is indication of the difficulties faced by the Rosicrucian hierarchy. (For this hierarchy cf. p. 244.) The brotherhood which has placed an imprimatur upon this treatise and which herein is directly responsible only for the four lines appearing upon page six specifically suggested Max Heindel. This is outside testimony since this group of brothers have no part in the Rosicrucian responsibility. Despite an appreciable false exaltation of the man and an indiscreet and foolish comparison with one certain other teacher on the part of Mr. Heindel's followers the Rosicrucian Fellowship today (1925) reveals the most consistent carrying forth of the faith to be recognized upon invisible planes under Ural-Altaic auspices. *The Rosicrucian Cosmo-Conception* remains the most widely circulated and read volume and so the most influential outgiving of the school. This is the only possible identification as modern prophet of the triad. Cf. following foot-note and Ural-Altaic, p. 228.

[2]For Ezekiel cf. p. 228. Astrologically and superficially this

cycle is marked by the cooperative movements of Saturn and Jupiter but in human affairs the periods as in the case of all solar cycles are dramatized at the corresponding equinoctial and solstitial points of the sun's revolution. Max Heindel quoted instructions of his teacher to the effect that a nucleus philosophy had to be given out before the close of the first decade in the century and a temple established before the close of the second. (The Fellowship published dates are inexact to the extent that 1909 is considered the close of the first decade but 1920 of the second.)   Saturn and Jupiter are the planets of initiation and their principal cooperative cycle for the solar mysteries measures to 128 oppositions or the duad of balance raised to its heptad or seventh power. (Cf. foot-note[3] p. 128 for a brief demonstration of dimensional evolution.)   In a roughly approximate measurement which reveals the cycle the oppositions occur every twenty years and in sixty return to a given sign but in the next succeeding decanate so that with the corresponding conjunctions the duadic aspects take place in ten-degree divisions of the zodiac at ten-year intervals and thus lend significance to the decanates.   The point at issue when this century began was the literal salvation of the solar mysteries.   (Cf. foot-note[2] p. 185. The preservation of the spiritual nucleus was necessary to avert a cataclysm which in 1874 seemed inevitable for 1926. Cf. foot-notes pp. 238[2], 242[2].)   Any existing order in cycle measurement must be intensified at its next-to-last point if the new order is to be born out of it at the time of completion. This required the fulfilment of the Ezekiel cycle at the 127th opposition and conjunction respectively.   In 1910 the opposition occurred on November 18th in the significant first degrees of two foundation signs and so brought the critical decade to a cyclic close at the winter solstice of that year. The conjunction which astrologically did not take place until September 10th, 1921, similarly corresponds to Christmas in 1920 at the time when the Fellowship temple actually was dedicated. The hieratic purpose of this temple has no particular connection with the Fellowship's healing work. (Cf. foot-note p. 125.)   For the 127 oppositions the mean interval between these aspects of 19.74 years is taken which produces 2507 years and this added to the calling of Ezekiel to Babylon in 597 B.C. measures to 1910. Here is the inaugural cycle in the present Aryan epoch for the first solar mystery-teachings and for their last recapitulation. Similarly the destruction of the temple at Jerusalem in 587 B.C. and the establishment at Oceanside 2507 years later is the corresponding or related cycle of the inner work. (All B.C. dates are largely approximate while modern planetary tables are only appreciably accurate but the cycle indicates itself clearly enough to identify the true nature of Max Heindel's work. Cf. preceding foot-note.) The reestablishment of the formal solar mysteries is indicated by the 128th opposition in 1930 for the public teaching and by the corresponding conjunction in 1940 for the dedication of the sacred city. The actual dates probably will center around the winter solstice in the first case and the vernal equinox in the latter.

CHAPTER V

THE DIMENSIONS OF BEING

BEING IS PERSPECTIVE

HE fifth key truth is important because it is adjustive. Upon a primal duad of time and space and through a resulting duad of form and consciousness all things possess being. The nature of the ever-illuminating distinction between consciousness or substance in process of growth and being or the fact of sentience as a quality of mass is expressed in this key truth. The literal constitution of being is in consciousness yet the first and constantly underlying subtle life activity that is the reason for sentient outer expression can only receive the term for basic reality of existence or be identified as being itself.

Being is perspective because it is known through activity, substance and form in relationship to itself as the differentiated center or individual absolute in creation. A myriad other differentiations and individualizations exist but in each case these are perceived by a given form of intelligence through the being which has created that intelligence. God in ultimate constitution or the chaos of eternity and God in absolute expression or the divine spark of

144

differentiated being is one God and a unity whole and indivisible. Cognizance can no more be traced inwardly to the absolute than outwardly to the ultimate of all creation.[1]

The identity of the tiniest basic atom with the immeasurable cosmic void may be sensed as a geometrical unity in the divinely perfect sphere pattern. Tiny and immeasurable are comparable adjectives of outer form. They express a separative attribute of the divine that has no function in cosmic reality.

An excellent mental gymnastic is this teaching which in its very awkwardness aptly clutches at the greatest of all truths. The ultimate atom of matter contains a complete universe and the greater universe of which life is a known part is a gigantic atom coeval and identical with every one of the chemical basic atoms which constitute it.[2] Distance or lineal dimension is the most active single contributing factor to the illusion of objective crystallized being. The divine is geometric always. The measure of deviation or of separation from primal reality is in form the descent of the sphere into solids and plane surfaces and is in process the interruption of cooperative fluid cycles through cosmic domain by crystallized duration fields of activity limitation.

[1]Behind the bridge of the nose is a sinus which holds the invisible atom of individual being in solution. To the highest of clairvoyance this space is shadowed or opaque and even in an undeveloped individual is impenetrable to the greatest powers of white or black magic.

[2]The belief that each fundamental atom contains a complete miniature solar system is now general in material science.

Consciousness is the constitution of being but is neither the support nor the fact of existence. All mass possesses consciousness of some sort and degree but the phenomenon is merely a signature of inner activity in its substance. Consciousness regarded as the reality of being and synonymous with the latter term[1] is a superficial truth accepted by many present-day schools of occult philosophy. No conception is more hampering to an orderly mental conquest of supersensual realm and function.

Consciousness indeed may be taken as being itself and so analyzed but the universe by such a method is broadened out into that rambling incomprehensible sweep to be noted in a conventional and convenient acceptance of physical space as the abstract possibility of extension. Space becomes baffling in its infinitude. In the supersensual realm of the psychic world the physical fourth dimension becomes a cosmic fifth through which all infinite boundaries of the present material universe are extended out into incomprehension by an increase in the proportion of the infinitesimal chemical atom of substance to the whole sphere of the physical cosmos. To this nightmare of distance and size is added the possibility of compound proportionate increases in abstract extent brought about by the sixth and seventh cosmic dimensions.

Through a reverse philosophical process an at-

[1]The growing and deeply rooted view of modern agnostic philosophy.

tenuation or projection inward to incomprehensible infinity of division may be achieved. Not only has science divided and redivided its atoms, molecules and electrons but savants have philosophically rediscovered the energy atom of the ancients or the basic chemical microcosm and have carried it through succeeding divisions of its supposed self as instruments and research with growing success have permitted the probe deeper and further into infinitesimality.[1]

Modern medicine has isolated the germ cultures of most diseases and through them has developed a method of palliation by antitoxins.[2] Upon this achievement the whole western world has built up a fear of tiny microbes barely visible to the most highly powered magnifying lens. The average individual firmly believes that a dozen or so of these are able to destroy the bulking universe of a man.

Popular occultism has reflected this tendency in its consistent fear of floating thoughts and of invisible entities. Many students will give to a wisp of astral substance clinging to a drifting action-pattern from the lunar plane the power to incite man into acts of self-destruction or to force him against his will and his divine inheritance to follow any

[1]Present civilization has been passing through this general scientific period of mental focus upon the tiny in reaction from the Neo-Platonic and Middle-Age gropings outward into bleak deserts of amplitude.

[2]Stated as palliation rather than cure because occult philosophy knows that accentuated germ culture is the disease itself and so never the cause.

caprice of this unensouled decaying no-thing. An otherwise normal human will shudder at the impact of a thought and will through a particular ingrained belief in the potency of infinitesimal things rest helpless before the suggestion or else seek assistance in charms, *mantra* and such protective herbs as the friendly garlic of the Mediterranean peasants.[1]

But distance whether in light-years or in micrometric subdivisions and size either atomic or in multiplications of the mass and volume of heavenly bodies are both matters of that linear measurement which contributes most to material illusion and which after all is two-dimensional and so only of use in detailed mundane matters or in attenuations of time and space through form and consciousness.

Being is perspective or the geometrical awareness of which consciousness is a support and expression. Consciousness or any other faculty when carried out indefinitely reaches objective infinity. Sight carried too far or fixed too steadily upon any near object blurs into non-sight. Hearing cannot meet the linear test of distance or of duration and the other senses fail similarly. By concentration the very con-

[1]The coddling of neurotics which is common in occultism has obscured the real nature and danger of the obsession against which garlic is still employed. True obsession can result only from astral leprosy in rather a progressed stage and as such it requires the sanity in isolation and protection with which the modern world meets physical leprosy. In the western world any danger of leprous infection is slight to the negligible point and the likelihood of obsession is only little greater even in a present age centered almost wholly in astral excitement.

sciousness loses itself whether in projection or in the attempt to hold to a given subject fixedly.[1]

Reality is that universal coordination embodied in the golden truth of occult philosophy. Being is the center both conscious and unconscious of all such relationship. All fundamental cooperations radiate from being in perspective or point of view.

In terms of this perspective all relationship relatively is simple whereas mensurally it may seem to reach infinity and to extend beyond. In the fascinating problem known as the quadrature of the circle the ratio pi[2] between the circumference and diameter may be carried out mathematically to millions of decimal points without the achievement of an exact figure. A regular polygon of any number of sides may be inscribed in a circumference but no addition to the number of sides actually will create a circle although in sensual reality such increase approximates the result. The factor pi may be used as 3.142 or 3.1416 for all practical purposes. The coordination in practice between circumference and

[1]The device by which supersensual development is achieved in the East. Consciousness is driven out to make room for transient illumination rather than raised in dimension to hold eternally the divine awareness.

[2]3.14159265358979323846264338327950288419716939937510582097494459230781640628620899862803482534211706798214808651328230664709384460955058223172535940812848111745028410270193852110555964462294895493038196442881097566593344612847564823378678316527120190914564856692346034861045432664821339360726024914127372458700660631558817488152092096282925409171536436789259036001133053054882046652138414695194151160943305727036575959195309218611738193261179310511854807446237996347496735188857527248912279381830119491298336733624419366430860021395016092448077 etc.

diameter is simple enough for any non-mathematician to understand while similarly no inherent abstruseness exists in the principles of occult philosophy when they are considered through proper perspectives.

Truly no fog of the incomprehensible is offered humanity by the supersensual philosopher. The divine is not infinitely distant but rests ever near. God is not the ever receding mathematical quantity of *pi* but is the sphere of the aspirant's own being bisected into expression by the diameter of simple individual relationship.

Being is not separation in dimension but is rather the fact of unity in geometrical cooperation. Being is perspective.

THE OCCULT CONCEPTION OF VEHICLES

The supersensual philosopher approaches analysis of sentient expression[1] through a careful distinction between the form and its central atom, divine spark or ego. Form is the balance of forces through which the atom of being is manifest in objective existence and so is the pattern in carrying specialized substance or the vehicle[2] of an ego.

The consistencies of matter and the concurrent existence of substance in several domains provide the groundwork for an occult understanding of vehicle. Material mass may be mineral, vegetable, animal or human. The higher includes the lower. Human

[1]The detailed consideration of the following chapter. Cf. p. 167 ff.

[2]Indiscriminately termed body, vehicle, sheath, principle or nature in popular occultism. Cf. foot-note p. 69 for distinctions.

constitution or consistency summarizes in function all processes of specialization up to its point in evolution. In their lesser complexity of constitution the animals similarly include both vegetable and mineral kingdoms while the plants embrace the simple earth substance which alone is subordinate to them.

The first distinction in vehicle is through extent of domain. Physical atoms are each ensouled by the tiny egos of mineral consciousness but an association of these lowest specializations of primordial mass in mundane substance must be attracted as a group in order to provide a vehicle for an ego of the next kingdom. The additional central spark of each of these first gropings in material sentient life constitutes the focus of being in a higher consistency or domain. The group-ensouling vegetable spark is first centralized in a nucleus that has no existence in earth substance. It is a seed-atom of the higher life stream. It incarnates in a small sympathetic cluster of mineral atoms and through that initial nucleus attracts to itself and concurrently releases from its being the elementary chemical forms in a regular process that becomes life.[1]

The vehicle created by this first cluster increases in extent to embrace a greater and larger number of atoms in the subordinate domain proportionately as the central spark or ego gains in sentient or conscious experience. The first distinction in vehicle

[1]In man the traditional complete change of physical atomic substance throughout the body every seven years.

results from the fact that each physical atom has its own ego or soul and yet if specialized into higher kingdoms in addition temporarily and during its tenancy of a form of superior domain has that which is not a part in the being of the seed-atom ensouling the higher vehicle but is rather a share in the consciousness engendered by life processes of such a superior form in which it becomes embodied.

As man subconsciously contributes to the higher spiritual processes of world and cosmic evolution so the egos of subordinate kingdoms serve him in his vehicles.[1]   They are as unconscious of his being as he in turn is unaware of the true spirtual life to which he adds.

Human individuals may and do often affirm their presence in the invisible body of the Christ or planetary spirit.   Tangibly the statement has no meaning because the fact possesses no direct physical experience.   Only in the ability of the faithful to sense an additional spiritual essence flowing through their own material being is any awareness of the constant universal eucharist to be gained.   For the average Christian it must be dramatized upon Calvary and in the mass or communion.

The simple basic relationship of atom to man and of microcosm to macrocosm has been analyzed.[2] Upon the complex constitution of being in form and upon the multiple activity of this same being in con-

[1]For the vehicles of man cf. Appendix B, p. 255.
[2]Cf. p. 123 ff.

sciousness must now be built an understanding of the higher-vehicle seed-atoms in their responsibility for subordinate kingdoms and in their activity by associations of units through the different domains. The point of view is from the center looking out upon being's larger aspects.

Hitherto the entire consideration of the key truths has been through the cosmic perspective of specialization.[1] All things have been identified in various differentiations of creative activity. The concurrent process of universalization throughout the manifest universe has been considered casually and secondarily.

Hereafter the first specialization of the great in the small or the adaptation of particular form to special function must be taken for granted and therefore treated incidentally. The entire cosmic scheme of spirit's attenuation for its crystallization into matter becomes of contributory interest. With being or the inner absolute as the focal point of perspective all further analysis must be through universalization or that raising of lower form to higher function which is known as evolution.

The primal duad of time and space and the succeeding duad of form and consciousness together end abstract occult philosophy. They introduce the twin binary schemes of concrete life analysis first of which is being and expression or the duad of inherent

[1]This inversion in point of view is not to be confused with a prior change in perspective. Cf. foot-note[2] p. 126, also p. 116 ff. For specialization cf. p. 109.

activity and second of which is evolution and manifestation or the duad of conscious activity.[1]

First distinction in vehicle is by its extent of domain. Second is through its degree of reflexive response within the complete body of which it is a part.

Here is the full surrender to the concrete. All four vehicles of the normal human ego are equally active in any point of view from the orderly cosmic scheme. But through actual life in experience of being this inward balance is seldom found. The extent of man's deviation from normal is a measure of his individuality commonly marked by his emphasis of one nature or of one principle over another. The individual is a mental, emotional, sluggish or stupid type depending upon the prominence of conscious activity in some particular vehicle.

The phenomenon of this varying degree of emphasis demonstrates a stage in being whereby analysis may be removed wholly from abstract realm. Being as a mundane fact is simple existence and but slightly distinct from basic consciousness. But being as momentarily focused in activity through one or the other of the vehicles of man becomes sensual intelligence and this is mind or that lens of awareness which possesses greatest importance throughout occult philosophy.[2]

[1]Being is the consideration of this chapter while expression, evolution and manifestation in order are the subjects of the three chapters remaining.
[2]Most of the organized occult movements attempt in one manner or another as their principal work a conquest of this mind in man.

Being is passive perspective. Mind is perspective active through being. Being is simple sentience or is sheer existence. Mind is conscious cognition.

Mind itself is neither one of the vehicles nor a set faculty of mental consciousness but is a movable factor between the ego and each or any one of the ego's vehicles. Mind is only coincident with the mental nature in ideal situation.[1] Mind is being when and where being is attentive and it may be permanently focused as low as in a moron's infant prejudices. Mind is being in emphasis through the substance of consciousness in any particular domain and it may alter its position quickly and frequently.[2]

THE DIMENSIONS OF BEING

Being is perspective. The dimensions of perspective are created in recapitulation. Repeated actions apart from the reflexive cycles of instinctive self-maintenance are clues to individuality in direct proportion to their degree of repetition or to their recapitulation in parts and in reduplications of themselves. Through its repetitions the occult scientist diagrams and measures mind.

But as mind betrays itself through recapitulation so that very recapitulation first is necessary to produce and develop mind.

[1]The term mental commonly applied to world, plane and vehicle here reveals its particular awkwardness and ineptness.

[2]Mind as the power of sentience is in no wise synonymous with brain, disposition, instinct, intellect, intelligence, reason, sense, soul, spirit, thought or understanding. No word is so variously used in metaphysics. Through this treatise its employment is technical and is limited by its definition here in the text.

Impulse or ordinary reflex may result from simple being. As long as life exists in sentient form a manual impact upon any given spot will produce its particular automatic result which mind itself can hardly check. Not only in physical repercussion but in emotional and mental reaction this is true.[1] The instinctive impulse or stupid continued unvarying reflex in a given succession of circumstances is not proof of mind but of its absence. Intelligence but non-presence of mind is demonstrated by the professor who returns home at noon to change wet shoes and who proceeds to take off all his clothes and to get into bed.

Sensual focus is a matter of quick fixing of image akin to the light chemistry in a common photograph. This image of cognition is a pattern in consciousness substance. Repeated images strengthen the shadowing form but fixed focus blurs and destroys it.[2]

Mind is the fluid faculty of general consciousness.[3] Directed too constantly at any one point it erases itself and so produces insanity. Yet quick shifting of cognition from vehicle to vehicle without purpose marks the undeveloped and scattered constitution of subnormal individuals. Strength of

[1] Instanced in the success of the criminologist's lie-detector.

[2] A phenomenon of vibration already illustrated in connection with the physical sense of sight. Cf. p. 148.

[3] As a simple faculty operating alone it is the active sixth sense of humanity while intuition which springs from knowledge higher than the individual consciousness is prescience or in human beings a seventh sense.

mind lies not in its power of fixation nor in its opposite vacillating extreme but lies in its capability for recurrent and regular attention upon a given interest through a proper vehicle.

Recapitulation is a common phenomenon in all growth and physical constitution. Mind which employs recapitulative power for its development whether consciously or instinctively must first be created as an active faculty by rehearsal or preliminary activity in conscious repetition.

Nature provides this process in a growth of higher forms through stages which repeat the lower. The inner and controlling vehicle is objectively developed in the individual not first but last. Man in his inception is a protoplasmic cell differentiated from the beginnings of all sentient form only in the greater complexity of the cosmic pattern to which in abstract form realms his nucleus is linked. In the womb of the mother the human embryo passes through regular cyclic stages of organic life from the cell to the human form. Yet at birth the future individual is no more than the physical pattern of man.

To clairvoyant faculty the higher vehicles are revealed present with the physical but more slowly developing as they hover around and suggest a misty embrace of the form. As yet the child cannot function without them or through them. Mind or the active principle of being and general faculty of consciousness has still to develop into function.

But with birth growth at once sets in and until maturity the being of any human ego passes imperceptibly from a passive to an active stage through its living body which is at once mineral, plant, animal and man. The recapitulation is through four main cycles and through a subordinate exercise of focal activity within them.

No human being but at some moment in his life looks back upon his own past with surprise at a sudden new grasp or understanding of old problems and of earlier experiences. To him it seems incomprehensible that blindness now disgustingly obvious could then have been so unsuspected. Here is the phenomenon of mind growth. This is recapitulation through additional power of focus. The growth itself has been due to the very impossibility of maintained focal awareness in any set vehicle. Consciousness or intelligence has been distilled from being by the ability of mind thus to change its aspect and through such activity to deepen its focus.

The four main cycles of human growth to adultship are the familiar seven year periods[1] of infancy, childhood, youth and maturity. In each of these individual epochs the ego gains full control of an additional inner vehicle.

Through infancy the human offspring observes life in a shadowlike consciousness akin to the min-

[1]Traditionally an even seven years but physiologically the multiplication of half a puberty period which varies with climate. Quick development or long sex potency generally marks lesser complexity of being.

eral. The baby is capable of reflex and impulse and of some anticipative cognition of a higher order induced by its environment and through its partial association with higher vehicles which it yet must ensoul.

In the succeeding epoch of growth the child possesses mind in a first stage and so exercises mental functions through contrast of self-awareness in the physical vehicle with social awareness in the etheric double. This is a period of growth accentuated not only in the physical but also in that unclouded imagination which is the mark and prerogative of healthy childhood. "Let's pretend!" says the mind of the youngster and then by induction simulates an anticipative reality of all experience to come. While the child is not yet able to draw his higher vehicles down to that union of their seed-atoms with his somatic centers which would give him active control of them he is nevertheless fully capable of using a higher power in a reflective cognition which develops his consciousness.

Similarly the period of youth gives mankind a round seven years of general focal interest in animal or human passions and so of direct emotional experience. Maturity ushers in the union of being with that fourth vehicle in which mind normally and naturally should center.

This is the fourfold birth of occult philosophy. It is reflected in a quadruple death out of which comes the explanation of most modern psychic phenomena.[1] The years between these extremes measure the great span of man's conscious activity through which mind or the central general faculty of his being focuses and expresses itself in his various vehicles by haphazard or by orderly phenomena. These manifestations of mind are the dimensions of being in the objective world.

THE DUAD OF KNOWLEDGE

The machinery of perspective is facts. Without established objective relationships all knowledge would be traditional as it was in ancient days when philosophers were trained in the mysteries and had only the careful observation of their own experience and their own life period to use in demonstration and self-proof of the principles taught them. The long-established weakness of premodern occultism has been its unconcern with facts.

Present-day science is an outgrowth of Arabian mysticism and alchemy. In its research the facts are balanced against observed truths while only proved hypotheses are used to analyze the natural activities of inorganic substance and of sentient life. The foundation beneath this whole pyramid of knowledge built by savants in unselfish and painstaking labor is facts. Science itself is the tabulation not of the theories of mankind but of things definitely and objectively known and established. Its weakness has been hypotheses built with little concern in perspec-

---

[1] E. g. cf. type-shells or the discarded disintegrating higher vehicles of deceased egos, p. 122.

tive and with but slight interest in the power of the human mind.

The occult duad of knowledge is perspective added to facts. Realization of the importance of the former rather than the latter pole of this binary process is necessary for an understanding of occult philosophy. Facts do not change except in their aspect but perspectives differ in the case of every individual seeking knowledge.

Point of view is through mind focused in a vehicle. Perspective translates the message of the senses below and of the intuitions above into understanding and intelligence.[1] Yet a new devotee of occultism always is surprised when he tells or demonstrates his great inner awakening light to some one else and so discovers that his understanding is non-illuminating to another person. The true teacher is one who is trained to approximate in his being the mind focus of his pupil and who thereby is able to explain a principle in the terms of the pupil's experience or understanding. Community of mind is union of perspective.

Because of this necessity higher knowledge must be given to the public or to large groups in symbol and parable. In this text no departure is made from the universal method of the mysteries.

Definite pictures are built of the eight selected cosmic symbols given as time, space, form, conscious-

[1]Memory is specialization of consciousness stuff and so exists in every vehicle. It is in no wise a particular function of the mental world. Cf. foot-note[1] p. 155.

ness, being, expression, evolution and manifestation. Eight corresponding Pythagorean numerical ideographs of basic relationship are taken and in order compared with these cosmic symbols in the light of the reflection of both series in human experience. This is for the greater understanding of each series through the other.[1]   All of such interweaving is as truly teaching by parable as the tale method of Christ.   The value of the present scheme to this treatise is its closer approach in procedure to modern science.

The human mind is infrequently normal.   It is usually precocious or stupid and its whole make-up is the measure of its speed of cognition above or below the cosmic mean.   Seldom is the general focus in the proper fourth or strictly human vehicle.

Humanity possesses the power to descend truly to dwell in any of the lower domains of sentient life upon the planet.   As a physical and medical fact ossification may transform a large part of the living structure into crystallized mineral matter.   Similarly the cretins are pathological instances of humans wholly in the vegetable stage.   In lycanthropy the Middle-Age superstition gave form to the descent of man into animal consistency and this is not so uncommon a phenomenon as science believes.

[1]In the use of the Pythagorean symbols the duad is employed in particular through the chapters of the other numbers because it reflects and specially aids the process of extraction of knowledge from experience in a pole of understanding.   Cf. foot-note[3] p. 128.

Through all living human beings the mind approximates these conditions in a visible plane of reality.

The congenital idiots are merely beings without cognitive intelligence. Here the mind does not rise above the physical center in the body. Physiologically the condition is a lack of connection between the mineral and higher vehicles. The morons[1] in an approximate vegetable stage are more than a majority of the people of the western world since the general intelligence by scattered scientific tests would show an average age type of thirteen years. The etheric double is the normal domain in this group of human minds. The passionate group or those human beings in the approximate animal stage reveal correspondingly a phenomenon of mind commonly functioning in the astral nature. Only the thinkers of the world possess a normal balance in the lunar plane. They alone are able to sense reality in superorganic phenomena.

Yet the mind may be reflected upwards into a shadow awareness of higher worlds in the manner a child anticipates faculties he develops later. The process of enlargement of consciousness to permit higher focus of mind in true broader reality is known to occulists as initiation.[2]

The perspective of the seeker in any successful teaching of occult philosophy must be met upon its own ground and there alone guided to a true duad

[1] In the newspaper sense of congenitally thick.
[2] Cf. pp. 33, 248.

of knowledge. Otherwise supersensual truths or principles are accepted in a dream or shadow perception unsatisfactory in application and more than useless in a world of hard fact and of present reality.

THE SCIENCE OF SIGNATURES

Perspective is a thought microscope or telescope as the case may be. Mind is the lens that alters an image in perspective and thereby conquers the size and linear distance which are illusionary dimensions of the objective.

Occult understanding does not differ from any other sort of knowledge. It merely builds upon wider conceptions and therefore requires more accurate facts. Since in its basic structure this philosophy must eliminate size and all objective standard of dimension it is driven for its records of achieved wisdom to symbol and to abstract relationship represented in form and picture.[1]

The cosmic numbers, the space dimensions, the domains, the kingdoms, the life-streams, the worlds, the planes, and the vehicles are all symbols or active signatures of definite supersensual understanding. The day, week, month, year and other duration units in occult knowledge are patterns of activity that may be substituted one for the other and again are signatures in relationship. The sphere in mathematics and its counterpart in form whether as a whole or in curved surfaces and arcs of division are likewise to the occultist a key of understanding.

[1] Cf. foot-note[1] p. 39.

The position of functional centers or organs in the body and the shape or location of continents, mountains or oceans upon the earth alike yield signatures to the trained supersensual scientist.[1]

In astrology the signatures are of first importance. Aries as a sign of the zodiac is not a constellation that by some vague indefinable radiation of influence is apt to create a child with red hair and a big nose but is an occult signature of being marked in the heavens by the stars which happened at the time of charting to be clustered in the thirty degrees immediately following the vernal equinox in the ecliptic.[2]

All things everywhere are significant. In occult philosophy every classification of phenomena and every tabulation of knowledge is based upon these signatures. Form and fact provide the patterns and perspectives through which signatures are recognized.

THE TETRAD AND ITS SCHOOL

The Pythagorean four or tetrad is the number of crystallization and it represents the quadrants of being. It discloses the twin polarities of situation and activity and so the combination of two duads into itself or it reveals the triad of process to which

[1]The ancient doctrine of signatures was that all objects bore a mark suggesting useful application to human need. In occult philosophy the doctrine is enlarged by an application of the golden truth. All objects in their activity, substance and form indicate their relationship and thereby their usefulness to all other things. The indication of relationship is the signature.

[2]Cf. p. 63.

is added the monad of further dimensional evolution by which objective form and substance are together constituted in crystallization.

Cosmically the four is the atom or fundamental sphere. This is the addition of a quality of abstract form to the solidity of matter. Since the triad is simple activity the tetrad is the rooting of process in set recapitulation or habit. It is the sphere sense of self-containment.[1]

The school is Theosophy and the prophet Helena Petrovna Blavatsky. Her persistent emphasis upon facts in their inner relationships and her use of scientific and philosophic modern thought as the basis through which she gave out in her books a tremendous measure of traditional occult lore are characteristic of the tetrad. She was the first to insist successfully upon the occult truth that all fact and form in nature possess occult meaning. Single-handed she blazed the way for a new occult science in the western world and alone she leavened the whole spiritual outlook of the English-speaking nations.[2]

[1]Cf. foot-note[3] p. 128.
[2]Cf. p. 193.

CHAPTER VI

The Dimensions of Expression

EXPRESSION IS COOPERATION

HE sixth key truth is important because it is coordinative. Expression is the result of that being which is its complementary extreme in a polarity of inherent life activity.[1] Expression is always a definite signature of being.

Being is the individual absolute and must be first consideration in any quaternary analysis of material existence and phenomena. Objective being is built upon activity, substance and form which with the universal non-identifiable source of all have provided a preliminary supersensual but corresponding tetrad in this present outline of occult philosophy.[2]

Expression itself completes the initial objective binary manifestation of cosmic activity through creation. Here is the duad of balance and vibration by simple cooperation in sensual polarity. This duad functions out of and above that underlying triad of activity represented by the triangle of universal process inverted and so identified as the pyramid of ma-

[1]Cf. p. 153.
[2]The non-identifiable source in the first chapter, activity in the second, form in the third and substance in the fourth.

terial substance.   Expression is two upon three or the pentad as well as a sensual duad.

Therefore the five objective senses are paired. The eyes, ears and nostrils are two each.   Taste divides the mouth into twin areas consisting of the alert taste-buds at the tip of the tongue and the less acute remaining group which again is paired.   Touch presents the nerves of superficial and of deep sensation or of cold and heat respectively.

Expression of the ego outward to other egos is the simple pentad.   The necessary duad of sensual cooperation is represented by the pole of communication between sender and recipient of an impulse. The five sensual expressions remain single and are form or physical conscious objectivity, aura or etheric emanation, odor or psychic catalysis, movement or lunar plane reflex and voice or creative articulation.

Directed inwardly all sentient expression is inherently dual.   The balance of cooperation through which come coordination and comprehension must be provided through the actual structure of the physical organism and to that end the senses are paired to fit them for their subordinate function[1] as outposts of

[1]Balance or general bodily equilibrium is a subordinate function of the ears through the etheric circulation focused in the semicircular canals.   Music alone has direct influence upon the higher vehicles and may even be employed to quiet the insane through direct impression upon disconnected principles.   Revelation or general expression of the ego in passive being through body processes is a subordinate function of the eyes in association with the alimentary-urogenital system or metabolic circulation.   The eyes are

consciousness. But of principal importance is the unipolarity of the entire body. This is an emphasis of poles which alternates in individuals so that the present human life-stream and all advanced lower orders may be divided into two great primary objective classes of male and female.

Here is sex or the universally possessed duality of sentient constitution. Lower orders not objectively so differentiated are bisexual and contain both poles actively within themselves or are asexual and display that unorganized duad of cooperation noticeable in simple cells which spontaneously divide by fission.

The symbol of man's conscious objective beginning is Adam who dramatizes in occult tradition the division of an antediluvian hermaphrodite human shadow-form into male and female. The pentad is sex or monadic individuality springing from fourfold being. Sex objectively is added to supersensual evolution and becomes the separation of man from God

the windows of the soul which cannot be masked. Resonance is a subordinate function of the nostrils through the sinus chambers and is associated with volitional expression and the muscular-nervous system or neural circulation of the body. The seed-atom of volition and of all being is therefore cloistered in an upper sinus. Poise is the subordinate function of the flesh and skin as the sense organs of feeling. This is the systemic precipitative and absorptive circulation associated with the lymphatic system. Through the skin the spiritual tone of being is instantly betrayed to the sight and touch. Appetite is the subordinate function of the sense of taste and is focused in the vascular-pulmonary system and the blood circulation. This life urge is the basic expression of being and therefore in conventional occultism the blood is given as the vehicle of the ego itself. These five subordinate sensual functions or circulations are the five solar breaths known in Theosophical teachings as *yvana, samana, udana, prana* and *apana* respectively.

in order that the life-stream may be constituted in material reality through a polarized physical form.

The latent quality of each sex is subjectively active in the other and thus produces physical affinity. All sensuous expression is dual and fundamentally sexual through the higher if not the lower centers of the body.[1] Even spiritual ecstasy is highly phallic and first was known in the ancient ceremonial orgies.

Sex therefore is expression in polarity or is objective aspect of being determined by and in cooperation with an opposite. It is the form relationship of positive, male and objectively emanative qualities to negative, female and objectively receptive qualities.

Expression is cooperation because it is the means of objective binary activity.

THE OCCULT CONCEPTION OF COORDINATES

The very foundation concept of occult philosophy is the principle of universal coordinates. This is embraced in the golden truth. All things are related and so coordinated to all other things in activity, substance and form.

Coordination is the process of discovery or creation of harmonies between any two or series of things that can be brought into comparison. It is most conveniently illustrated by a kindergarten method.

Two apples, two pears and two paper bags by numerical coordination are six objects. The addition of eight people to the problem creates fourteen separate things but enters upon a matter valueless and

[1]This is the libido of the psychoanalyst.

of little signification in itself since nothing essentially alike or common exists in a group that can only be known as a total of objects. In occult philosophy the bare total of things is a dimension of abstract extension akin to linear distance and to objective size and it is inherently useless. All units multiply and divide themselves into infinity on very slight provocation and the mathematics which interprets relationships alone contributes to supersensual knowledge.

But the eight people all possess a general liking for fruit which then becomes a coordinate factor since four items of fruit can each be cut into halves to supply the eight by equitable division. The paper bags have no interest coordinate with their contents and may be destroyed. If peaches should replace the pears the problem is somewhat complicated by the additional difficulty in dividing a stone-center fruit neatly while if small ripe plums should be substituted their division becomes so unsatisfactory that an advantageous solution of the problem might be to cut up the two apples among six individuals and to distribute the plums whole.

All this coordination is based upon an assumption that each of the eight people would be satisfied with any part or piece of the division. It develops that three out of the group wish apples and four of those remaining prefer plums. Only the non-committal individual and the three apple zealots are destined to be satisfied. Out of the four who would like plums two must be persuaded to accept a share of the apples and for this purpose these members of the party must be subjected to analysis in smaller spheres of reciprocal relationships so that the divergent factors of appetite and fruit may yet be reconciled satisfactorily.[1]

Here is illustrated the process of coordination. A start is made in the simplest or most attenuated sphere. Fourteen things do not coordinate because they have no community of identity except as units of useless mass number. But with four pieces of fruit and eight hungry individuals a satisfactory distribution is only a matter of transforming simple differences into harmonies to be found through considerations added successively.[2]

The occult interest in coordinates lies not in matters such as this adjustment of action to circumstances but rather in an understanding of significant activity and form types through analysis of the cooperate relationships and exciting or retarding antipathies that have produced them. Objective expression never results from accident nor from unrelated creative forces. The abstract quality known as appetite was a coordinate which related people and plums. This same appetite is the sole cause of objec-

[1] A child for instance may be subjected to discipline and ordered to take a piece of apple or a youth in self-sacrifice might defer to the wish of a hypothetical sweetheart.

[2] A fundamental principle of metaphysics is that human consciousness cannot possibly dislike that which it truly understands. Any matter may be resolved to a satisfactory state. In the *Codex Occultus* this is the law of gravitation in the quality group of the chemical key under the heptad.

tive maintenance of being in a sentient universe and is the keystone of a scientific material doctrine of survival in function and species.

Coordination is intellectual simile or metaphor but only in abstract philosophic realms. It is symbolization or dramatization but in an occult sense. Literally it employs definite signatures of the existence or activity together of things in equal degree or similar relation.

The procedure is demonstrated in astrology. The signs of the zodiac correlate to the pattern and condition of things and the planets to the active forces and processes. Leo[1] in the body rules the cerebral hemispheres, the pineal gland, the corpus callosum, the optic nerve, the heart, the spine and the whole of the back above the diaphragm. The sun which as a planet is the traditional lord[2] of Leo controls the life or being itself, the volition, the coordination of function and the chemical creation of the necessary carbon compounds of body tissues. Leo and the sun are not merely symbols and signatures of these things but are highly useful coordinates in the sensual mathematics of occult philosophy.

The machinery of expression in metaphysics is nec-

[1]Leo is the first sign of the invisible spiritual zodiac. Aries as the fifth sign clockwise from and including Leo is the head of the terrestrial zodiac for the present fifth epoch while Libra as its opposite is momentary regent of the cosmic equinoctial point.

[2]Lord is the astrological term for an inherent relationship between the processes and conditions to which any planet and any sign may respectively coordinate. The one is strengthened and the other intensified by the presence of the planet in the sign.

essarily arbitrary while the conventions of identification are themselves never the truths they express. In its employment of simple signatures occultism merely places metaphor upon a scientific basis.[1]   In this conception of coordinates the supersensual philosopher only employs a scientific simile to give himself thereby an enlarged language of idea.

THE DUAD OF EXPRESSION

Actual expression of being is to be recognized in the simple duad of the nature and duration of things.

The nature of expression is the determining factor in dimension of being through form.   Thus in activity all expression is process or progressive proceeding and change.   This creates the active relationship between prior and subsequent condition which is known as the present or essential nature.   Since this present activity considered by itself cannot be measured in a duration which emphasizes its impermanency it must be considered in form or that fixed image of the moment which is susceptible to analysis.

Observed form changes its nature constantly in response to shifting relationship. It compares differently with its own prior and subsequent states, with its own superior and inferior environments and with comparable forms associated with it in its own immediate sphere.   Sex is the set objective polarity of most sentient form yet even in physical functioning this is variable.   Philosophical sex or positive and negative quality in all chemical composition is not-

[1]Cf. p. 164.

able for its extreme of change in relationship. Few substances can be found that while generally masculine are not feminine to a series possessed of greater positive nature than themselves.

Sex broadly considered is the constituting factor of the nature of things. It represents the process of individualization that is responsible through polarity for all evolution. In objective form this polarity is noticed first in constitution and then in relationship. Through gradations of positive and negative reaction the nature of any form is determined and diagramed.

The duration of expression is the determining factor in dimension of being through activity. Objective expression is cooperative in form, situation or circumstance. Cooperation is not process itself but the result of activity. The triangle of time analysis permits the present or point of analysis to be compared with the past in consideration of that which contributes or adds to the expression and to be compared with the future in consideration of that to which the expression is directed and must lead.

Here is the basis of the houses in the astrological wheel. The four angles are a cross created by polarized duads erected at right angles in the two separate but blending cosmic and mundane spheres.[1] The midheaven is the positive and its opposite is the negative pole in the plane of meridional or spiritual activity while the ascendent is feminine and its opposite

[1]Cf. p. 63.

masculine in the creation of vibration through the plane of horizon or earthly manifestation. From these angular houses the full twelve are created first by trisection of each quadrant and secondly through a geometrical triad of activity which relates each fourth preceding and each fourth following house to an angle. The tenth house or indicator of business and social situation has contributing to it the sixth or place of the balance in service that will be received from or must be given to others. In turn the tenth contributes to the second or house of financial accumulation and of all result from business or social effort.

The duads of expression interweave to create the active pentad of the Pythagorean system.

Either the inherent nature or the inherent duration of things considered as a duad is taken at one pole to form the focal point in a triad thus momentarily constituted in cooperation with the other two poles.[1] For while both sexes as an example grow

[1]The abstruseness here is only apparent. (Cf. foot-note[1] p. 222.) Two narrow slips of paper may be taken to represent the two duads. The slip to indicate the nature-of-expression duad should be marked "objective" (positive or masculine) at one end and "subjective" (negative or feminine) at the other. The slip to indicate the duration-of-expression duad should be marked "specialization" (cadent or contributing) and "universalization" (succedent or resulting). The slips may be laid upon the table as a cross to show the cooperation of the duads in any tetrad of form. Similarly they may be laid in the form of a tau in any one of four possible combinations. Each pole of each duad in turn may be subverted by its position in the junction of the arms in the tau in which case its own nature is lost in the creation of the active triad while in its superior and additional duadic activity with the focal point of the triad it adds in a new twofold element and creates the pentad.

through experience only one may enter the triangle of duration in any given case. While a man may continue to blow hot or cold he cannot do both simultaneously and so individually and objectively must remain either male or female. Similarly form in that duration which individualizes or specializes being must through alternate emphasis upon expression in polarity through positive and negative states hold to a relative fixity of type and pattern or summarizing situation. Only that sentient form thoroughly set or crystallized in order or species manifests objective sex types.

The pentad of expression results from the natural activity of that duad only concerned through one of its poles in the underlying triad. In polar emphasis of inherent nature the superior or pentad activity is the manifestation of the latent sex. A male individual gains power in expression through development of receptivity on all planes while a woman achieves expressive power through growth in resistence to external physical or supersensual influences.[1] In polar emphasis of inherent duration the superior or pentad activity in expression is the particular emphasis of specialization and contributing

[1] The vehicles of the individual alternate in polarity so that this latent activity is principally accomplished in the etheric and mental which are of the nature of the latent sex. It is best induced by the superficial repetition and imagination exercises given by most modern occult schools to inner students. The alternation in sex of the vehicles in an individual is the necessary cosmic reversal which marks adjacent grades in the states of separation between spirit and matter. Cf. foot-note[2] p. 126.

tendencies or of universalization and resulting tendencies. Man as a race or simple abstract being as a manifestation of the absolute progresses through the latent specializing tendencies in general universalization or through the latent universalizing tendencies in general specialization. This is respectively the involution and evolution of occult philosophy[1] and is an eternal binary process of duration that gains power in direct proportion to increase in the fixity of form.

THE CODEX OCCULTUS

The *Codex Occultus* is an orderly presentation of the fundamental principles of being. It is not a unique or an only canonical code but is one of many developed by man in his regular evolutionary cycles of understanding. It is as comprehensive a scheme as can serve useful purpose in modern study of life phenomena and yet interpret the primary and underlying causes of creation.

In form it is a series of laws. These are not the particular consideration of this treatise which is rather an introduction to the *Codex Occultus* and so an exposition of the principles upon which it is built.

In structure the *Codex* represents an extension of the method used throughout the organization of material in this present work.[2] But for the larger collation of definite natural laws a more fundamental device must be employed than the eight cosmic sym-

[1]The consideration of the following chapter. Cf. p. 192 ff.
[2]Cf. p. 161.

bols here selected for illustration of the unfoldment in dimension of cosmic process.

The dimensional unfoldment itself continues best interpreted to human understanding through the cosmic numbers now universally identified with Pythagoras[1] but to be found in the remains of earliest human philosophies whether in the actual number-names preserved in their digits by the Mayas of Yucatan or in the geometric signature teaching of the first Aryans and the corresponding zodiacal knowledge of the Egypto-Nubians.[2]

The whole organization of astrology as well as the divine geometry developed in the ancient mysteries is built fundamentally upon the numbers. To the zodiac in the heavens and to the great sphere of a geometrizing god man looks for his deepest wisdom. The decad and its ten digits underlie and explain these and so constitute the very ultimate of abstract philosophy. The highest conceptions of divinity emanating from the human consciousness are numerical whether unity or trinity or else the mystic Tetragrammaton founded in the fourfold form of the four-lettered name which in English is known as Jehovah.[3] Even the sacred ten or decad is the

[1] Termed Pythagorean throughout this text as a matter of convenience.

[2] The fifth family race of the Sabians which survived into historical times through the Memphite or earlier priestly hierarchy in Egypt. The star worship of these early philosophers has left its impress throughout the Near East while the Memphite priests invested with magic the very names Egyptian and Chaldean. For Sabians cf. p. 235.

[3] JHVH, JHWH, YHVH, or YHWH.

divine quaternary number of the Pythagorean system since there it results from the addition of one, two, three and four.

The *Codex Occultus* is built upon the Pythagorean numerals as are the key truths. But to the first eight of the series running from the cipher or oudad through the seven or heptad are added three remaining numbers of importance not considered in this treatise. These are the eight or octad, the nine or ennead and the summarizing ten which is the deuteromonad or decad.[1]

In the present introduction to the *Codex* arbitrary cosmic ideographs are used to illustrate and to give a sense of the foundation numbers. But time, space and the other six are after all no more than symbols of understanding. In codification of occult natural law the procedure must take in advancing cross-sections of unfoldment the numbers of divine constitution as revealed through an effective interpreting agent. For this purpose the actual facts and phenomena of life must be used in order to create the logical poles of comparison. Simple life in its utmost of specialization and of objective being is the natural opposite to the universal and subjective divine which alone is representated by the numbers.

Given facts of life could be taken separately through the unfoldment of dimension which represents inherent numerical constitution but the work though accurate and illuminating would be colossal

[1]Cf. pp. 85, 252.

while the task would be endless. Therefore occult philosophy turns to a device nearly as old as the Pythagorean numbers themselves or to the traditional seven great keys to knowledge established with the solar mysteries. These are cast into a comprehensible modern form.[1] As a series they conveniently represent the full sum of possible points of view or perspectives out of human experience and so each in turn may be carried through the full dimensional series. Every point of contact establishes between first cause and last result a principle of cooperation that becomes a small group of natural laws which in this definite limitation of sphere may safely be put into words. As drawn together and classified these foundation principles are a contribution of modern supersensual philosophy to an embryonic occult science. As so orderly arranged they constitute the *Codex Occultus.*

The seven keys possess a septenary manifest form but nevertheless are truly a function of the pentad or school of inductive analysis. Thus are seen three duads that naturally correlate as pairs and an additional key which serves actively to interpret the inner relationships of any one duad in cooperation with either of the remaining two. This seemingly lone key which is the second is therefore considered after the other six.

The microcosmic or solar key is first and it establishes the laws of force or pure numerical coordina-

[1]Cf. Appendix C, p. 256.

tion.   It is called the microcosmic key because it deals with fundamental universal relationship from the perspective of a center taken in the first cosmic expression of being.   The great habitation of space is specialization of mass objectively far removed from divine first cause.   Yet creative emanation is constant or eternal and for analysis must be taken at a stage where general universal complexity has yet to complicate the process.   Such a center is to be found only in the individual absolute or that reflection of the greater sphere which eventually duplicates every larger procedure and which to occultism is known as the microcosm.

The laws of reflex and the principle of emanation as represented in Pythagorean number are the particular realm of this path to knowledge.   Through simple association the fundamental forces are identified.   The key is also known as the solar because the cosmic processes represented in the primal evolution of an individual are reproduced dramatically in a larger sphere by avatars or the conscious incarnation of deity in a great world teacher or in a Christ.   Material science recognizes here a recurrent solar myth.   The set necessities in the public life of such an individual beginning with real or assumed virgin birth and ending with actual or simulated violent sacrificial death are merely historical rehearsal of the principles discovered in natural law and made clear through the first key.   The solar myth is the true pattern of all initiation.

The third key is the macrocosmic or lunar and it deals with the dimensional laws, the zodiac and world evolution. It is the companion key to the first since both of these approach understanding of all things through an analysis of cosmic process. In the little man or microcosm the larger sphere is only reflected yet in the human individual the macrocosm may be studied in its initial stages or unfoldments in exactly the manner that the human embryo is used as a key to the biological history of mankind. Such a method alone gives little more than a theoretical understanding of the larger universe but with the facts of separate beginnings may be contrasted observations of the outer sphere as it exists and reflects its own inceptions through its processes of growth.

This is accomplished through the zodiac or heavenly man. The individual upon the earth is essentially a pattern of the cosmos and the heavenly counterpart is a divine type-form in his superior celestial domain. The zodiacal man as a microcosm in that greater immeasurable stellar universe is macrocosm to humanity and thus names this key. It is lunar because in occult tradition the moon contains and reveals the sum of the earth's past growth and experience and so to man is the distributer of *karma*. These lunar and macrocosmic laws of dimension when reflected in the vision of what should be through the solar knowledge and initiation are the guide to all situation and to all relative condition.

Identification of mundane matters in the zodiac and measurement of mundane circumstances in heavenly movements are the sure interpretation of complex cosmic actuality.

Fourth is the musical or key of vibration concerned with the movement of matter in its adjustment of mass to mass and of force to force in inherent relationship. Here is the harmony of the spheres and the demonstration for the golden truth of occult philosophy. This is the first of two keys that deal with creation as an objective fact and not as a process. Tangible reality is upon this path of knowledge a clue to the divine. The laws of geometry and the natural affinities of vibration through chords, tone, color and sensual awareness contribute understanding of the purposeful activities in all substance and form. As in music any discord may in the hands of a master be built into harmony created through some larger concept of melody so through the musical key and its geometry are all facts of existence resolved into useful coordinates upon some cosmic orderly plane.

Fifth is the chemical or key of transmutation that deals with the laws of phenomena and with the objectivity of all force, mass and consciousness. Material matter is chemical in constitution. The crystallization of anything in the universe into tangible form or activity is a matter of ultimate chemistry. The laws of phenomena interpret the power of objective existence. Consciousness is substance and truly chemical. The first faint divine emanation in a cosmic night gains chemical actuality before its force can be known or its work proceed.

The musical key adjusts objective actualities in tangible circumstances or situation by the interpretation of their external relationships. The chemical key explains all objectivity of any sort by a resolution of outer constitution and activity into the essentially chemical processes responsible. Chemistry is the key to inner particular and eternal verities.

The seventh key[1] introduces the physiological path to divine illumination. Through understanding of the human body is gained the greatest and most complete source of occult knowledge.[2] The temple of the indwelling spirit is unlocked to the seeker through the laws of development and so by analysis of function and consciousness. The seventh key involves the usual life cycle familiar to human consciousness in its own experience. Its method of study is by comparison of ordinary function with the result of deviation from normal in the enlargement or degeneracy of activity in any part of the body or through the laws of consciousness and also by observation of the relative physical positions and interchanges of cooperation between the many different parts of the body or through the laws of anatomy.

[1] Taken in precedence of the sixth.
[2] The oldest method continuously used in the present epoch since it was employed by the pre-Aryan Egyptian hierarchy and through them transmitted down by physical succession to the present Rosicrucian initiates. This slender and very frail thread of the mysteries has never been broken.

The seventh and sixth keys provide a duad focused immediately between the duad of cosmic analysis or consideration of space from its largest possible aspect and that of matter constitution or consideration of the cosmos in its most attenuated crystallization. In this focal duad sentient experience and living phenomena are first taken into account. Life is the result of cosmic evolution and of chemical matter. Both these factors are dependent upon consciousness and upon the development created by the universal presence of life in the cosmos.

The phallic or ecstasy key is the sixth. It creates the laws of divination and provides through correspondences the easiest and most practical path of all to occult knowledge. It is the key of the abnormal or orgasm life cycle. It is based upon the ability possessed by living structure to create small anticipatory cycles of sensation or activity and through them to reflect larger and infinitely slower curves of experience.

Sex phenomena and spiritual exaltation are but a small part of the field covered by this key of intensification. Individualization in all life and recapitulation in all function contribute to the correspondences.

Second and last of the seven is the biological or history key which is built upon the laws of process and upon the abstract principles of specialization. It is the third life consideration or the classification of recapitulatory processes whereby form and function evolve to their highest point of usefulness or specialization and yet it is also the guide to interpretation through the augmentation or decrease of process in cosmic and matter analysis and so is associated intimately with all four other keys.

It is the historical key since facts contribute to it whether of geology and archaeology or of man's social and political struggles and their outcome at any particular age. Because its field of activity is in laws of process it controls that knowledge always held most sacred in the ancient mysteries or the great secret cycles.

INDUCTIVE OCCULT UNDERSTANDING

Occult understanding is not itself a code nor a creed. It is not available in any form of recitation or affirmation since the individual absolute is unique and different in at least some one phase of expression from every other single spark of the divine.[1] Within the inner comprehension of being lies the lens of mind which transmits awareness into knowledge but experience grinds no two of these lenses precisely alike.

Were this not true the whole orderly emanation scheme of divine evolution through separation would fall. Understanding is individual by cosmic necessity. The whole purpose in rehearsal of fact and in ritual of expression is hardly to implant knowledge

[1]The fact that no two sets of finger prints are identical is simple demonstration of this.

which seldom can be done but is rather to assist all inner comprehension toward general wisdom.

Traditional occultism teaches that during those ancient epochs when mankind in evolution was childish occult facts were dogmatically stated. Neither induction nor deduction was permitted nascent intelligence. Individuals who demonstrated precocious flashes of understanding were killed promptly to prevent the spread of any general inclination to stray into dangerous fields.[1] Knowledge was quarantined because at that time man possessed no consciously controlled sentient vehicle with which to draw it into his own being and comprehension. Every possible device was employed to force growing humanity to take seriously its new crystallized life in a world illusion. So states tradition!

This was anterior to the mysteries and is a true description of cosmic process in somewhat too literal terms.

Deduction followed dogma and was the method used to cultivate understanding under the sway of

[1]The death of Socrates who was not an initiate for inadvertent betrayal of secrets of the mysteries is a popular puzzle in modern occultism. Actually Socrates died because his mood denied him acceptance of the graceful escape laid open for him. His defense forced the Athenians to make good upon their gesture and to vote his death. Here was the hand of inner *karma*. Truth on the one hand and the balance of human evolution on the other protect themselves through the sheer momentum of being. Destruction of misguided leaders and teachers is never deliberate nor cold-blooded but is merely the abandonment of the stiff-necked to their fate. The brotherhoods never seek to enforce punishment but have wisdom sufficient to incorporate their requirements into the normal trend of natural law.

the lunar temples.   Truths were symbolized while inferences were encouraged.   Every natural force was deified.   All sentient form was given person and intelligence.   Evolving men and women developed imagination or a first stage of understanding because the trees of the forest spoke to them and because the winds and storms that swept down the mountain sides were divine agencies at which they could tremble.   Each house had its spirit and every village its god.   Dreams were presentiments.   Not a tangible reality in life but that from it human intelligence at this period did not deduce and infer latent fundamental cause.   While the symbolization was crude and the resulting superstition black the process was sound and evolutionary.

Induction is the method of the solar mysteries and is the foundation of the splendid modern sciences they have nurtured.   Material philosophy has broken at last the tyranny of authority and the yoke of empty revelation.   In occultism the teacher ordained under the solar knowledge never cites nor gives his authority to establish a point but quotes only in illustration.[1]   Modern science in its great clarification of human knowledge discards every belief and hypothesis which it is unable to demonstrate at will either in the laboratory or through the experience of each investigator.

The inductive canons[2] are seldom employed liter-

---

[1] A consistent complaint against Christ in the Bible narrative.

[2] The methods of agreement, difference, concomitant variations and residual variations.

ally yet in principle they represent the full process used in acquisition of scientific understanding. The seven keys are worthless in dogmatic application and actually of little use in deduction or inference. Their power may be perceived only by each seeker within himself when taken by him inductively and so used as a convenient device for holding the investigating reason and the sensual observation to a particular intellectual domain.

THE PENTAD AND ITS SCHOOL

The Pythagorean five or pentad is the number of expression and the principle of induction. It is the two of cooperation upon the three of activity.[1] It is the monad of actual emanation in the objective realm built upon the tetrad of crystallization or of constitution within that realm and through an increase in cosmic number is the usual additional abstract dimension which gives out of the four the Pythagorean five in ensoulment or space consciousness and which further in this resultant broader understanding reveals the reason for expression.

The school is Science and the prophet is Francis, Lord Bacon. Bacon has been given universal deference as the father of modern philosophy and as the author of the modern scientific method. While savants do not and actually never have followed the principles laid down by him nevertheless he is truly entitled to the position given him by posterity. His insistence upon vigorous exclusion and elimination

[1]Cf. p. 167.

together with his regard for tangible observable facts as the basis of all intelligent observation was the foundation and cause of the modern world's great successful revolt against medievalism or authority and tradition unsupported in experience.

CHAPTER VII

THE SCHEME OF COSMIC EVOLUTION

EVOLUTION IS ADJUSTMENT

THE seventh key is important because it is reflexive. It turns natural process inward to reveal nature through herself. It summarizes the first one of a last pair of considerations in this treatise and thereby introduces concrete life analysis through the duad of conscious activity which is evolution and manifestation[1] Evolution is adjustment because it is the definite process of universalization or adaptation of lower form to higher function.

Evolution is not a haphazard development of sentient being in response to environment and inner appetite nor is it a spontaneous generation of life phenomena through the action of chemical laws. Objectively these are correct deductions of truths grounded in the tradition of occultism. But when modern science remains aloof from subjective factors of cause and direction its great thinkers must necessarily accept conceptions of an accidental rather than an orderly universe.

[1]Cf. p. 153.

Epigenesis or the development of new forms by simple growth out of old ones is merely an elementary truth of physical phenomena. Preformation is a false doctrine of evolution only in so far as scientists look to the physical seed cell as the germ of being. Modern material philosophy has learned that it must seek outside and beyond the chemical man for its explanations of human complexity. Environment and heredity insufficiently account for fundamental divergencies of character while epigenesis which proved untenable as an explanation for the descent of species has likewise become unacceptable in its larger hypothesis of spontaneous cosmic generation.

Certainly it is true that types develop strange offshoots. Yet a larger understanding of contributing causes serves gradually and surely to resolve all oddity into regular greater cycles of influence.[1]

The veriest child in modern scientific knowledge knows that if dust accumulates in some rocky crevice the combination of sun and moisture will produce living growth. This is not spontaneous generation because the earth particles attract and carry tiny seed cells and is not true epigenesis since this new life is never apart from an invisible pattern or form to be found objectively and identified somewhere else. The creation of a planet in the heavens with the prompt appearance of life upon it as it cools off is

[1] Illustrated in atavism or Mendelism and in inductive astronomy by the discovery of Neptune to account for the aberration of Uranus.

perhaps more suggestive of an unplanned haphazard sentient beginning but only because the cycle and sphere are large and because comparison with other worlds and domains of sentiency is impossible.

All earlier theories of cosmogony were based unconsciously upon the assumption of a nature ever prodigal or of a creator generous in his wasteful strewing abroad of every opportunity and blessing. Science and religion have cooperated in this training of human comprehension into a fundamental error. As men were believed left adrift by God and thought to be gathered into the fold of grace solely through the chance discovery of an only salvation and the accidental moment's mood which would determine a favorable reaction to this message of atonement so the whole world was conceived by thinkers to be some sort of monstrous divine experiment or some equally bizarre chemical curiosity.

In recent years science has uncovered gradually the true economy of natural process and law while the Eastern wisdom has crept into occidental consciousness with a necessary message of divine conservation and utilization of soul material.

Chemistry has shown the atomic construction and basic indestructibility of matter while physics has demonstrated the eternal persistence of force. Through the human body medical science at last has realized that nature is far wiser than intellectuals who rush into print to interpret her or to lay down laws for her guidance.

Within a generation great surgeons have taught the utter uselessness of the vermiform appendix, the pineal and pituitary bodies and many other parts of the human frame. Now anatomists know that the removal of the appendix mysteriously retards intestinal function and that the supposed survival of atrophying organs in the ductless glands of the midbrain is instead the presence of controlling centers for the major chemical processes of growth and molding of body tissues to pattern.

Research has developed the modern endocrine and hormone hypothesis to account for mysterious powers of tiny parathyroid and suprarenal wart-like structures within the human form. Excision of all the former produces death through violent convulsions in a few hours while the injection of extract from the other restores life to the seeming dead. Goiter is not now taught to be merely the dilation of a useless gland nor do the testes and ovaries serve alone a sexual function in medical theory.

Vitamin is a new word coined to explain the inherent intelligence of human appetite. Investigation found that man did not thrive on a rigidly scientific diet but regained normality when given articles which apparently possessed no food value at all. This was first believed merely a matter of excitation of gastric juices by palate pleasure but eventually the tests demonstrated the presence of a hitherto unknown effective agent. Thus the efficiency of nature has gradually established itself through several generations of scientific thought and now is enthroned as the necessary basic fact in all functional investigation.

The presence of a bone, organ, gland or odd cell specialization of any sort in the human body means not the passing away or atrophying of an element no longer necessary to life but rather the presence of a usefulness yet to be demonstrated. Investigators at last realize that visible evidence is no necessary proof of function.

Evolution truly understood is the adaptation of both form and function to enlarging purpose and expression. It is based upon the fundamental specialization of life cells in which each one individually surrenders many or nearly all of its activities in order to develop outside itself and beyond capacity of its own sphere some particular process of life in cooperation with the grouped cells of the larger domain. This may be the building of general tissue for the creation of form and objective being or may be the further intensive individual activity in the function of some organ. Throughout this process the cells adjust themselves to their environment in the tissues that contain them while the certain groups further adapt their activity for the purposes of higher evolution in the whole sentient form.

Function is the process of evolution. Evolution is adjustment. This key truth is guide to an understanding of all life activity in tangible form and being.

THE OCCULT CONCEPTION OF DUAL TENDENCY

Nature is eternally efficient and economical. She neither develops sentiency through spontaneous generation nor higher form through accident of environment or surface condition. This is the fundamental understanding of natural law from which alone can come any synthesis of science and religion. Here again is demanded consideration of more than the physical constitution of things.

Occult philosophy has taken the word involution and has given to it an enlarged meaning[1] to cover those cooperative processes in subjective worlds which in material domain result in evolution. Through involution and evolution the supersensual philosopher establishes a basic hypothesis of metaphysics known as the occult conception of dual tendency.

All active process is orderly as it must be from necessity in a coherent cosmic scheme. The apparent disorder through wide evolutionary tendency may be transformed into understanding by the warp-threads of whole fabric relationship. Form itself may be analyzed through the simple duad of specialization and universalization operating concurrently in cooperation.[2] The cosmic processes through

[1]With the special sense here in almost as wide and common usage as astral. One text-book with twenty-six thousand copies sold (1922) indexes this word so used under eight subject-headings and thus provides an interesting commentary upon sleepy lexicographers fooled by the general illiteracy in the modern occult field.
[2]Cf. p. 111.

which form exists may similarly be diagramed and reduced to comprehension through the interweaving of evolution and involution.

Involution is not so much a reverse of evolution or a prior series of steps down which life has trudged for a present reascent as it is an inversion or complementary pattern on invisible planes of the outward and directly determinable evolution. In a broad sense involution reveals itself in specialization as evolution similarly results in universalization. Yet specifically the terms universalization and specialization must be applied to the substance and form of external crystallization while the new duad here introduced is applicable only to the sentient life principle.

All duad analysis is through simple cooperation and must be limited strictly to the boundaries of proper domain. Basic mineral matter can hardly be said to evolve in its specialization through the imprisoned cell structure of higher form although its evolution is aided. Neither is the evolving ego or spark of man and animal universalizing in chemical decomposition or the liberation of mineral kingdom substance from body cell atoms. Evolution proceeds through an enlarging of coordinate function and constitution in the whole life-stream.

Animal egos in contact with man are highly specialized through reflective acquisition of individual traits and through consequent restriction in type. Yet these egos evolve only in their own order when no longer subject to higher sentient influences. This is shown in the tendency of any animal to revert or degenerate to its type as an individual while the species still continues its slow evolution. Horses or dogs which have been domesticated for thousands of years become wild and almost untamable during separation from man less than the length of their own generation.

Plant and vegetable life similarly is cultivated by human kind into species adapted to particular use and is through metabolism further specialized into the organisms of both higher kingdoms. But this cultivation and specialization do not mark its evolution. The reversion to type of grains is indicated in the failure of domesticated varieties to perpetuate themselves when growing wild. Root-crops cultivated by man since savagery are more or less poisonous when undomesticated as in the case of the sweet potato and in a majority of instances require the action of fire before the pulp is edible.[1]

Objective specialization always aids evolution but it particularly indicates the complementary involution which is an equally constant and ever present process. Involution alone permits the attenuation of cosmic influence in a more specialized domain for the purpose of evolution.

Man molds animals by domestication, plants by cultivation and minerals by use in field and by manu-

[1]Tapioca which is possibly the oldest adapted food of mankind was first made from a cassava root that contains raw a deadly amount of prussic acid.

facture. Human individuals by association with superior orders of intelligence similarly further their
own specialization.

In the dim antiquity of occult tradition the divine
hierarchies were tangibly present in the objective
world to guide and domesticate nascent involving[1]
humanity through its golden age of slight personal
responsibility. For higher spiritual development
man still requires this cooperation which now is
achieved by initiation and by membership in some
one of the invisible brotherhoods.[2] He is still subject to racial and national influences that are the
active and tangible specializing forces in the world.[3]

In conventional occultism these higher-kingdom
principles are taught through the symbol of racial

[1]Since the separation of the sexes man's net evolution has been
focused in the individual and therefore the prior life-stream evolution upon the globe is commonly called involution. This involution is a process which still persists and which results in the op-
pressive crystallization of race and the depressive overspecialization in group degeneracy that together force the individual to be-
stir himself through his latent divinity.

[2]Membership in an invisible brotherhood is achieved by demonstration of an occult usefulness and by acquisition of a cosmically necessary task. In literal terms acceptance can be described as an automatic procedure which involves no secrecy whatever. Neither vows nor literal obligations exist. No objective ceremonies are necessary although they accompany the event in the
case of a neophyte guided into illumination by any society established upon the physical plane.

[3]This explains the baffling complexity of every civilization which
first through guild movements trains its crafts and then through
a commercial structure increases human necessities to a point that
overtopples the culture. The versatility of individuals first looked
upon with suspicion and then accepted through the decadent period
in an increasing degree is transmitted to the capable individuals
of the entire group in the ultimate but always partial salvage of a
civilization.

and national guardian angels or of ensouling spirits
for the larger groups in each of the four kingdoms.[1]
Individual man who is objectively crystallized and
specialized by his environment and circumstances
yet progresses constantly as a unit of divinity. This
individual growth not only is added specialization
but it is universalization and its sum through the
race is the net evolution of man or the balance in
adjustment between forward and laggard members
which again is an illustration of the key truth. Similarly domesticated animals and cultivated plants stimulate species evolution. Environment and circumstances are the production of the higher-dimension

[1]Racial or group spirit is a figure of speech for a recapitulatory
differentiation in the sevenfold emanation of function. This differentiation exists at a stage between the individual and the whole
life-stream and is analogous to the etheric plane constitution existing in recapitulation between the physical and astral worlds. In
the subempyrean orders the angels may be correlated to man since
they are individual in the physical realm, the archangels who are
planetary egos may be correlated to these group spirits whether of
man or lower order and similarly the lords of mind or motion of
the Rosicrucian teachings may be correlated to the life-stream as a
whole. Here are merely expressions of the balance point in contributing lesser dimensional stages known as the Diana period
(For periods cf. p. 204.) for the angels, the Janus period for the
archangels and the Saturn period for the first emanation or Logos
here termed lords of mind or motion. The thrones, dominions,
virtues and powers are the Christian orders of first unfoldment in
greater dimensional stages while the principalities correspond to
the lords of mind. (Cf. Appendix A, p. 254, and the gradation
of occult orders, p. 243 ff.) The study of these superior evolu-
tions is only valuable as an exercise in analogy. So far as any
actual or useful knowledge possible to man is concerned the group
spirits are unconscious and in objective expression represent mere
distribution through natural law of the sevenfold cosmic nature.
The attempt to escape group-spirit domination except by long initiation is idle.

group spirit or of the pattern involution which permits the complementary development marked in the individual.

Evolution is social[1] or is the whole considered as the result of the usefulness of parts. It is the process sustained by basic form. Involution is separative or is the parts considered as contributory to the whole. It is form set and established by growth. As specialization and universalization are concurrent processes so are involution and evolution.

Involution is passage from diffusion to concentration or is the subjective descent of spirit to germinal form. Evolution is the derivation of all form of life from earlier and simpler type by gradual modification in response to this descent of spirit of higher and greater consistency. Involution cooperates with the evolution which alone can be analyzed in practise. Evolution in analysis is the state of development or growth as compared to other states.[2]

In occult philosophy the dual tendency of all things is organized through evolution or that state which is defined as the collective relationship of the condition and result of any process to the circumstances of external and internal existence. From state or focal position in being all activity is considered as concurrently influential in two ways or as positive and negative, objective and subjective, specializing and universalizing, evolving and involving.

State itself becomes the prime consideration in

[1] Cf. p. 123.
[2] For the various states cf. Appendix D, p. 257.

analysis of that focal position which is being in manifestation.[1] Chemical factors will create a solid, liquid or gas out of any particular composition but these vary with every condition whether of temperature, air pressure or inherent quality. Of concern to the occultist are the abstract relations of general state known as solid, liquid or gaseous and identifiable only in objective comparison. The solidity and gaseousness of a compound and not its substance are of first importance. Through this succession of stages is achieved the triad of activity.[2]

The scheme of cosmic evolution numerically is twin triads represented by the interlaced triangles[3] widely known as Solomon's seal. This is the hexagram which was the symbol of the Pythagorean school and today is to be found not only in the monograms of occult societies but on Hebrew temples.

In the conception of dual process every triad of activity is complementary to a companion and together they manifest each of the many duads. Any process for a complete understanding must be analyzed by three stages taken in two directions from the state or position of analysis. Each stage upon one side of a diagramed focal position must correspond to that stage in the same position away from or towards the focus upon the other side.[4]

[1]The entire consideration of the following chapter. Cf. p. 217 ff.
[2]Cf. pp. 140, 176.
[3]A triangle is a symbol of the triad of activity rather than a literal diagram of threefold force.
[4]In the *Codex Occultus* this is the law of reflection in the recapitulation group of the phallic key under the triad.

This is the breaking open of the pyramid which lays bare the square of understanding.[1] The eight lines which bound the mystic figure become twelve as the four triangles are separated at the apex to stand erect pointing upward each upon its base. The active introduction of the triadic element permits the circle of twelve celestial mansions to operate and so provides the first approach in a grasp of the secret occult cycles.

THE SCHEME OF COSMIC EVOLUTION

The three traditional septenary schemes to be summarized in illustration of the sexenary[2] process of evolution through the ternary stages upon each side of a focal state are among the most commonly familiar and wide-spread teachings of modern occultism.

The initial series is purely philosophical and cosmic. The earth is taken as a type of definite evolution through universal domains. This scheme of seven stages marks the simple unfoldment of primary cosmic emanation that embraces the full life of Brahma from initial stirrings in the darkness of chaos through final dissolution of all creative manifestation and it identifies the chains or periods.[3]

[1]Cf. p. 6.

[2]Septenary schemes are subject to analysis under the hexad when the consideration is any activity in a succession of stages. The fourth or focal position is the perspective which momentarily must be ignored. Cf. foot-note[3] p. 128.

[3]Theosophical and Rosicrucian nomenclature respectively. The Rosicrucian considers this scheme in terms of succession and ignores planets other than the earth while the Theosophist analyzes the process in terms of position and therefore considers the planets

These states are named after the principal Roman deities who were Saturn or the ancient Italic god of seed-time and of the golden age of innocence, Janus or the Italic primordial deity of objective beginnings and of wisdom under the sun which he ruled, Diana or the ever-loved sylvan goddess of the moon and childbirth, Tellus who symbolized the earth from which man looked backwards and forwards in progress and understanding, Jupiter or the supreme tutelary spirit of the Romans and the god of heaven or the next life condition, Venus or the Latin goddess of Spring and so of new cycles and initiation and Vulcan or the Sabine god of fire and of inner consuming divinity.[1]

The periods[2] of Saturn and Vulcan, of Janus and

but ignores prior and future conditions. Neither word possesses dictionary authority in this usage and the latter must not be confused with the geological periods to which only a far-fetched correspondence exists.

[1]At a later time the sun, moon and earth were substituted as names for the Janus, Diana and Tellus periods and so have been taught in modern Rosicrucian societies. This has led to confusion through identification of these cosmic states with the planets in astrology. Particularly has this been so since some occultists have divided the earth period into Mars and Mercury halves to produce an aberrant correspondence with the days of the week and to symbolize man's first emphasis of force and his later employment of intelligence. In astrology the only correspondence by name in period and planet is through Saturn. (Cf. Appendix D, p. 257.) Note the Mars-Mercury controversy among Theosophists as further fruitage of confusion. (Cf. foot-note[2] p. 241.) The usual Rosicrucian nomenclature except for this confusion does no real harm in a modern world unacquainted with the genuine cosmic symbols embodied by the ancients in their gods.

[2]This Rosicrucian word is used because its emphasis is more accurate. Elsewhere the Theosophical terms are employed. Cf. foot-note[3] p. 208.

Venus and of Diana and Jupiter correspond. Processes which were subjective in the Saturn age will be objective in a Vulcan period. Involutionary or specializing tendencies of the Janus age become evolutionary and universalizing in a Venus period. Man who was a child of mother nature under Diana will through Jupiter-period tendencies learn to father and to give conscious creation to every natural process and cosmic form.

The periods as simple emanation or cosmic unfoldment are the links between external creation and the great worlds and domains of consciousness. Occult philosophy symbolizes this process by its teachings of successive rebirths of the terrestrial globe upon an arc or dip from higher to lower and back to higher worlds.

It is a scheme analogous to human fourfold birth if the involutionary and precedent process is prefixed to human incarnation by consideration of man's concurrent higher vehicle development.[1] The fourth or human principle which enters the body last comes first into being to draw the human divine spark down as far into objectivity as its own rarefied substance will permit. Around this nucleus is attracted astral matter for the animal vehicle which leads in turn to the tentative creation of an etheric double by incitation and to the eventual establishment of the focal physical form which coincidentally and meanwhile has gone through the lower evolutionary recapitula-

---

[1] An example of the employment of twin triads. Cf. p. 157.

tory stages from seed-atom to protoplasmic cell and from embryo to infant. After birth the etheric, astral and human vehicles in turn become consciously a part of the being. Human birth might therefore be described quite logically as the journey of the ego in descent through three worlds to a focal lower fourth and in ascent through the same worlds as the consciousness mounts up slowly to its proper domain for human expression. Through all the intricacies of occult philosophy the clue is remembrance of the warp-thread in a fabric. All processes must be taken out and drawn away from their normal activity and for analysis and understanding considered as separate phenomena. Yet everything in nature and in space exists and is active at once and concurrently. For man this present cosmic period is the Tellus but for his etheric double it is the Diana, for his astral envelope the Janus and for his own principle the Saturn period or first general consistency.

The Saturn and Vulcan periods mark consciousness of the earth in the spiritual world, the Janus and Venus periods identify activity of this globe or its inhabitants in the cosmic ocean while the Diana and Jupiter periods indicate expression of the planet or anything upon it in the great astral domain. The Tellus period serves as the focus or state of present general objective condition.

The periods therefore symbolize states of the progression from birth to death of the physical earth successively in various stages of consciousness and chemically are exactly analogous to the states of space.[1] The second traditional septenary scheme found in the rounds or revolutions[2] is analogous to the planet's sleeping and waking stages. The rounds[3] reveal a cycle or dip of succession through states of constitution.

The rounds are more than a smaller recapitulatory cycle of the larger process because in addition to the monad of simple arc through the triads in greater domains this consideration involves the duad of each world division into planes. The periods are merely the basic dimensional consistencies of space located by domain. The planes of the great worlds are the expression of the polarization in process through each of them. The periods identify cosmic condition whereas the rounds indicate cosmic activity. In the manner that condition is indicated by consistency activity is graded by density.

No nomenclature exists for the stages of density represented by the various rounds. Nevertheless as

[1]Cf. Appendix D, p. 257. More particularly and by an abstruse distinction the states of consciousness are substantive and interpret the Theosophical chain idea whereas the states of space are focal or formative and interpret the Rosicrucian period teachings.

[2]Theosophical and Rosicrucian terms respectively. Round is defined in the dictionaries as a Buddhist word while revolution must not be confused with the geological term to which it is broadly analogous.

[3]The Theosophical term is used because the Theosophical nomenclature possesses greater currency. The Heindel and Steiner text-books written a quarter century after Sinnett could have accepted the older terms as did Blavatsky and Judge or with minor adaptations as the chain-period of Leadbeater. In a modern perspective few of these changes have been felicitous. Cf. foot-notes pp. 127[1], 205[2] and p. 16 ff.

the periods exactly correspond to the states of space so the rounds may be expressed in terms of the states of matter.[1]   Noticeable and important is the pairing of these states in active duads.   Thus the solid and liquid states or the gaseous and etheric possess much less distinction between themselves than seems to exist between liquid and gaseous condition.

Within each round the dip or arc of that consciousness which is the human of the present epoch is traced by its position on a globe identified by letter.[2] D is the focal point between the series A to C and E to G. A and G are located on the lunar plane, B and F on the astral, C and E on the etheric and D on the physical.

A baby recapitulates lower form but yet in its conception is human and from the moment of birth displays traits of higher consciousness.   Its experiences in lower form are recapitulatory rather than actual. In the cosmic scheme this same necessity for lower experience from latent and higher point of view demands the rounds in relationship to the periods.   In each round in order focal consciousness moves from a globe to its successor as A to B while focal being remains constant on D.[3]

Superficially it might seem that these globes should

[1]Because the states of matter identify a stage of activity as the states of space indicate a stage of condition. Cf. Appendix D, p. 257, foot-note[2] p. 208 and trinity of being, p. 95.   For the states of matter cf. following section, p. 212 ff.

[2]By both Theosophists and Rosicrucians.

[3]Cf. principles of mind as means of consciousness growth, p. 155 ff.   This process is cosmic and so terrestrially inverted with the spiritual principle in lowest situation. Cf. foot-note[2] p. 126.

rest in the four great worlds rather than in the four
lower planes. This is apparently but not actually a
distortion of correspondence and is due to the cosmic dimensional decrease in any translation from
larger to smaller cycle. All space identification is
fundamentally a matter of dimension. The four
states of matter whether taken in one direction or
the other are entirely located in the physical great
world while the four ethers of occultism which are
corresponding states of consciousness are subdivisions of matter differentiation in a plane or polarized half-world.[1]

The conventional teaching of the periods frequently leads to a question of conditions prior to
Saturn's age or posterior to Vulcan. These periods
are dimensional and are not duration stages. On a
circle is neither beginning nor end. It possesses no
distinctions that are not relative. Before the god
Saturn was the investigator is. The first period
merely represents any extreme of understanding
backwards through one given condition of being.

The third traditional septenary scheme in illustration of the cosmic sexenary process is interesting because it is terrestrial and because man is not now
situated at his focal or D point. It is a typical

[1]The ethers are in reality seven as are the states of matter.
The formation of seven world divisions upon an addition of four
ethers to three states of matter is due to an incomplete dimensional
understanding. The three missing ethers are specialized by those
subempyrean orders which in the interests of clarity are ignored in
this treatise and are the G or consuming, the F or exalting and
the E or socializing ethers. They vitalize stages in the planet's
consciousness which are of interest to the initiate only.

scheme of evolution upon the earth itself in which
the present human life-stream is taken as a type
through the occult or continental geological epochs[1]
and is indentified in the root races[2] of humanity familiar in popular supersensual teaching.

Each root basic racial type of man is given a
particular alinement of terrestrial continents for development. The epochs carry the same names[3] as the
root races and are separated each from the other by
violent cataclysm but with a certain measure of overlapping duration through which is achieved an actual
interchange of blood stock that permits the growth
of a new race out from the one preceding.

The Polarian epoch showed a shadow mankind
clinging in an elementary recapitulatory existence to
land about the poles. The Hyperborean continent
which was somewhat similarly located later evolved
a second but still intangible stage. The Lemurian
continent and islands belted the earth at the equator
and there revealed humanity growing slowly out of
a low beastlike condition. Atlantis which was situated toward the middle Atlantic and spread out into
much land that is now Africa and the Americas first
cradled a real development of man. The Aryan or
present epoch is believed by conventional occult philosophy to be considerably past its central point and

[1] Another geological term adopted by modern occultism and used
in a very particular sense to which no dictionary authority has been
given.
[2] The root races are summarized in the following chapter. Cf.
p. 224 ff.
[3] Cf. Appendix D, p. 257.

to reveal now first signs of development towards a
new root race type.[1]   Tradition states that the
Aquarian[2] or sixth continent will center around present North America while the Hepatogenic[3] or
seventh root race will dwell in land which will replace Southern America.

Through this human racial development is shown
again as in all natural processes from the cosmos to
the atom a constant and orderly adjustment which is
evolution.

THE STATES OF SUBSTANCE

The states of matter are the basic or most common distinguishing limitation of abstract substance
and are based upon the fully crystallized or solid
form.   They are the adjustment of evolution within
a complete objective earth cycle.

The involving or specializing triad is familiar and
is recognized by science beginning with the etheric
or fourth state of Crookes and continuing through
gases and liquids to the solid state.

[1]Krotona, Mt. Ecclesia and Point Loma are three examples of
workers' colonies established in California because of this belief.
The latter two still (1924) are active.   California is generally believed by occultists to be a destined part of the new sixth continent.

[2]The next astrological age in the precessional scheme is marked
by the sign Aquarius in the zodiac.   The word Aquarian is without dictionary recognition in this sense but has caught popular
fancy and has therefore become largely current.   It is in reality a
misnomer when applied to the sixth race and to the corresponding
continent since these astrologically will be Piscian.   Cf. foot-note[1]
p. 173.

[3]Named because interstitial tissue in the liver is physiologically
the sign of development at this stage as similar growth in the
vermiform appendix betrays the Aquarian consciousness.   None but
the highest initiates display even the latter signature at present.

The occult philosopher uses evolving or universalizing counterparts which he conveniently designates as alcoholic, spirituous and rapt in correspondence to liquid, gaseous and etheric respectively. The physical extraction of essences or induction of consciousness is not an occult but is a chemical fact identified through the alcohols or spirits of alchemy and so known to science in phenomena if not in understanding.

The states of space constitute the fundamental unparticularized scheme of consistency through abstract substance marked in consciousness by the chains and periods of Theosophy and Rosicrucianism. They are naturally chemical in nature and are demonstrated in the chemistry of carbon or in sentient transmutation. Corresponding to the Saturn, Janus, Diana, Tellus, Jupiter, Venus and Vulcan periods they are the solvent, precipitate, sublimate, carbon, resolvent, catalytic and metabolic states of space.

In astrology these are the chemical natures of the planets and they represent the spectrum of graduated creative cosmic influence which is cooperatively and constantly active in human or in life activity and in terrestrial affairs.[1]

NATURAL SELECTION AND SPECIES

Classification is the great gateway to knowledge. Facts unrelated to experience are useless. The occult philosopher who by his conceptions is driven to

[1]For the three schemes of states cf. Appendix D, p. 257.

consider all known phenomena requires even more than does conventional science a constant placing of factors in order and species, in suborders and subspecies and in regular and systematic arrangement of relationships whether similarities or divergencies.

He recognizes occult signatures of inner present tendency in the selective operation of external conditions upon an organism and its parts. He sees therein the process whereby individual variation or variations that are of advantage in a certain environment tend to become perpetuated in the species. The survival of the fittest he knows to be true though not from the fitness but rather through the necessity of survival.

The supersensual scientist does not seek to discover new facts in life nor does he need new hypotheses. The method of occult philosophy is an enlargement in point of view and is a comprehensive presentation of principles which enable any investigator to classify all things and to trace out satisfactorily all relationships.

Order and species or race and type are the revelation in mundane life of cosmic geometry. Evolution and all development is self-consistent. As the birth of a great thinker may cause the world to tremble in terms of transcendentalism so any striking variation from pattern and normal tendency may require the cooperation of globewide cycles to produce it. Consciousness within broad domains brings by the very creation of phenomena a cosmic knowledge of each phenomenon's birth. Spiritual epigene-sis or the springing of something startlingly new from old cooperatives which neither contain nor sug-gest the innovation is a fact only when higher force intervenes in a lower sphere and when the result is considered without reference to the broader influence.

Through much of modern occultism is found the idea that man by his power may step aside from natural law and thereby do that which is unique and different. Truly he may merge his being into a larger cycle and even into one of his own selection and de-sire but his achievement great and divinely potent as it may be must still lie within the normal functioning of an orderly cosmos. Initiation is natural selection in supersensual domain.

THE HEXAD AND ITS SCHOOL

The Pythagorean six or hexad is the number of power and synthesis or is the two great triads of activity interlaced and cooperating in a multiplication of the three by the two. It is the pentad of expres-sion or induction with the monad of further dimen-sional evolution added in order to give force to be-ing and to create duration. It is the tetrad or the fundamental sphere of being considered through poles or opposites or an active duad linking the quaternary cycles of man and cosmos together.

The school is the Pantheistic or is nature and the prophet is Charles Robert Darwin who was greatest of all naturalists. While Darwin was neither the father of modern biology nor the most brilliant mind in anthropological science his epochal work upon the origin of species served forever to drive home both to popular and scientific minds the fact that nature herself in her signatures of life and form is the only possible storehouse of all knowledge and understanding.

CHAPTER VIII

The Scheme of Human Manifestation

MANIFESTATION IS FOCUS

THE eighth key truth is important because it is interpretative. Manifestation is the disclosure, display and revelation of the whole in objective being. The occult understanding of focus completes a grammar of cosmic language by supplying the detailed inflection of every unspoken creative word. Only the occult philosopher is in a position to function as interpreter of God and nature to human mind and intelligence because he alone considers the relationships of all things to all other things.

The individual who is student in this vast college of life must make a selection out of nature's curriculum and through appreciable periods of his development concentrate upon some department of knowledge until he masters it. Properly every graduate of the cosmic institution has achieved his bachelor's degree through specialization in one particular branch of wisdom. But while mastership is largely a matter of unremitting labor in some relatively limited field yet a broad general excellence in wider domains is required even of this advanced student.

The surgeon must possess some knowledge of medicine while the doctor's training includes several hundred hours in surgical anatomy.

One-sidedness is particularly fatal to supersensual development.[1] In present-day life the idea of specialization is so deeply rooted that the possession of any skill outside a man's trade or profession is regarded as legitimate matter for suspicion. Human beings discount versatility, fear originality and refuse to accept the unique. A person receives employment upon the basis of previous occupation and is generally refused even a trial in any new field. In amateur and professional sports a player is associated with his usual position. He is known as a short-stop or a quarter-back and is watched with keen apprehension in any other *rôle* of the team play.

The jack-of-all-trades subjected to condemnation in the proverb earned his ill-repute because he was master of none. Foundation skill or competency in some one line is expected to result from any human growth or progress. In social intercourse each man must yield justification for his place in society. "What is your line?" is a question which by decree of usage must always be answered. A name or symbol of being, a residence or sign of established place in the world, age or mark of general experience and profession or badge of active service in life together

[1]The occasional bizarre conceptions of modern occult groups once each leaves the narrow province of its own type are due to the refusal of practically all of them to accept truth or knowledge from any but their own sources.

constitute essential information about himself which
any citizen must give. The tramp and vagabond is
not expressing universal spirit but is rather demon-
strating an annihilative cosmic aimlessness which belongs to undifferentiated root substance and to
pralaya and universal night.

Man builds and grows upon his ability to add to
a social interest and central activity first earned and
established. All manifestation is built upon a center.
The great cosmic matrix sends out from itself all
subordinate radiations of relationship. An understanding of life and being in any broad aspect requires the mastery of one phase of knowledge as a
reference foundation and as a key basis of study but
yet also demands increasing competency in all other
fields and schools of truth. Synthesis is not a true
method for the study of truth but is always the result
and the unsuspected objective.

Manifestation is focus because being discloses itself from its center. Focus is centralization interpreted through the rays of specialization. Eventual
understanding of the whole of creative manifestation is the purpose for which the eighth key truth
may therefore be employed.

THE OCCULT SEPTENARY CONCEPTION

The occult hypothesis of manifestation is a universal cooperative septenary constitution in dimension and differentiation.

The sevenfold dimensional unfoldment is completed in the heptad and becomes the general cosmic

perspective of natural mundane phenomena. The seven differentiative rays of creative manifestation provide the means of concrete analysis of life expression through consciousness or sentient form and are the spectrum of being employed in the *Codex Occultus*.[1] Traditionally these rays are associated with planets and have long been known to occult philosophy as the Chaldean planetary order or succession which is employed through astrology for the measurement of cycles in stages of process. They provide the common rulerships of the days or hours and identify the valence or various properties of chemical elements.

The heptad is an outgrowth of the hexad through the addition of another cosmic dimension. The key truth of evolution turns natural process inward to reveal nature through her active self. This next convolution of numeral symbology yields an added understanding by an analysis not of the process but of the focus through greatest intensity of the co-operations between the threefold stages of preceding and succeeding activity. It adds this focal or septenary point between two triads and considers flat or static manifestation rather than involutionary and evolutionary relationship.

Here is consideration of sevenfold succession not as the arc or dip of process which involves the three comparative stages in a hexad of evolution and also the four planes or worlds of activity in a tetrad of

[1]The laws in the spectrum group of the musical key.

occult consistency but rather as the true heptad or objective focus from fourth position through the emanative spectrum.

Manifestation is that by which something is made evident to the senses whether it be the complete sensual universe or any part of it. Focus is the point of meeting of a system of rays or the place where an image is formed and a condition crystallized. Matrix is that which contains and gives shape or pattern to anything. Fourth position is the occult arithmetical matrix of all being. It produces manifestation by focus into form or eternal existence of the cooperative influence of three prior or contributing and three succeeding or resulting stages.

The occult heptad teaching based upon the sacred seven of the Babylonian founders of the present solar mysteries is the septenary conception of manifestation with seven rays each itself manifest in a fourth position in association with the other six, each inwardly complete in a sexenary scheme through its induction of the qualities of other rays and concurrently active in two complementary triad schemes of activity through the polarization or folding into a duad of the hexad comprising these other rays, each outwardly complete as that duad or the pole of active relationship which is created in the induction of the triad schemes in mutual cooperation upon either side of each ray through the establishment of the hexad and so also outwardly complete as a matrix of form or tetrad which is created by the addi-

tion to the first duad of a second general polarity between each individualized focal differentiation and
the whole heptad and each further through this individualized differentiation specialized in unity as the
monad and further universalized and socialized
through the pentad of expression which is established
by addition of the duad of individual differentiation
to either triad of process cooperatively active in particular expression and created in this activity by the
other duad of folding which completes the seven.[1]

The operation of the seven rays is most simply
demonstrated in the planetary succession or familiar
Chaldean order of astrology.[2]

The planets are taken in the order of their orbital
position in the solar system beginning with Mercury
and ending with Saturn. The asteroids are ignored
as well as any intra-Mercurial body or member of
the system from Uranus outward.[3] In fourth position the sun is placed as active representative for the
earth which in terrestrial affairs becomes the true
center of the universe.[4] The moon is the cast-off

[1]This cannot be made other than abstruse for casual reading
since more words would merely bury the thought while less would
lose it. Cf. critically foot-note[3] p. 128.

[2]Cf. Appendix D, p. 257.

[3]Actually twelve orbits in a broad sense are inhabited by planets
or their forming and disintegrating masses but only seven are ever
active in fundamental astrological constitution. Neptune does not
belong to the solar system but acts in cooperation with the sun in
a manner similar to the relationship between a planet and its moons.
Cf. foot-note on page following. In the terrestrial astrology the
moon is a precursor for Uranus but will not yield place to that
planet in physical matters until the reunion of the sexes in the late
Aquarian epoch.

[4]Cf. foot-note p. 67.

body[1] of the spirit now incarnate in the earth and as regent for transmissal of all *akasic* or negative influences is placed at the beginning.

Moon, Mercury, Venus, sun, Mars, Jupiter and Saturn become in that order the spectrum symbols for all differentiation of cosmic force in mundane life during the present Aryan epoch.

When these planetary symbols in order are placed around a circumference at even intervals and a seven-pointed star is inscribed in the circle by drawing a continuous line to every third planet the days of the week are obtained in the order of their rulership by the sun, moon, Mars, Mercury, Jupiter, Venus and Saturn. The planetary hours are Chaldean order reversed or the points around the circle which successively give Saturn, Jupiter, Mars, sun, Venus, Mercury and moon. When another star of seven points is inscribed by drawing a similar line to every second point the planets are placed in order by the atomic weights of the metals they rule from the heaviest or lead to the lightest or iron and so list themselves as Saturn, Mercury, sun, Jupiter, moon, Venus and Mars.

[1]The common teaching in popular occultism but a convenient rather than an accurate symbol and one quite awkward in the case of planets with more than one moon or with none. A better understanding may be gained in chemical terms if any lunar ocean or the joint realm of planet and moon be considered a cosmic storage battery in which the astral substance is the electrolyte existing commonly uncharged upon the astral plane but charged upon the lunar and in which the planet is the anode and the moon, moons or lunar vortex the cathode in the voltaic processes of this next world above the physical. Cf. foot-note[1] p. 232.

This regularity of position around the endless circle with the equal orderliness of cosmic measure obtained by subordinate regular intervals of exception demonstrates simply the arithmetical or spectrum heptad analysis in occult philosophy.

THE SCHEME OF HUMAN MANIFESTATION

The root races and subraces taught in the conventional anthropogenesis of modern Theosophical and Rosicrucian schools introduce the most fascinating department of all occult philosophy. Here is the scheme of human manifestation closely linked with the epochs and continents. These and the root races carry the same identifying names.

The story of the flood found in all ancient mythologies is the account of the last Atlantean submergence which was a typical cataclysm of the sort that mark the destruction of every decadent civilization and of its lands exhausted in human experience. A characteristic tradition embodying the inception of a new great root race is the Bible story in *Genesis* of Moses and his emigration with the Aryan forefathers out of the land of Goshen or a rich agricultural settlement in lowlands overshadowed by the City of the Golden Gates up through wastes now beneath the ocean to present Scandinavia and from there across wild northern steppes to plateaus surviving today as the desert of Gobi. By a method of record peculiar to ancient writers in the mystery schools the narrative is combined with historical accounts of captive Semites rescued from Egyptian slavery under the man who bore the actual name Moses. Since larger cycles and smaller mutually interpret each other the priests who were more interested in cosmic processes than evanescent human events built the stories into one in order to convey the lesson which man will sometimes learn from drama but never from history.[1] The plagues were historical happenings not in Egypt but in Atlantis where such magic was common.

The scheme in human manifestation is simple in thread but complex in the sense that it cannot be traced out as a whole in any single process of thought or study. The race form is the focus or matrix in manifestation of humanity yet is a threefold symbol rather than the set expression of mankind found in conventional occult and in all scientific teaching and speculation.

The races first in direct relationship to the epochs or continents are the successive stages in development of the present life-stream of man. These human egos or divine sparks entered upon their Tellus period as the Polarian root race of tradition and

[1]The *Gospel according to John* particularly illustrates how truth is enhanced by a dramatization in which the author throws off all limitation of literalness to concentrate upon accuracy of process and understanding. Historically it is the least faithful account of Christ since it contains many transpositions of events for effect. Yet of the four gospels it conveys the picture of real fidelity and the impression of the Nazarene of greatest use to seekers for divine truth. Cf. *Abraham Lincoln* by John Drinkwater for an example in a modern play of accurate portraiture gained by deliberate perversion in historical detail.

followed through Hyperborean, Lemurian and Atlantean to the existing stage. In the Aryan epoch now centered in Eurasia the dominant Aryan root race has recapitulated in its succession of differentiations objectively through the subraces which provide racial succession[1] or evolutionary adjustment to physical condition in the historical and actual material world.

The subraces are the Indo-Iranic consisting of Hindus and Persians; the Semitic embracing Assyrians, Arameans, Hebraeo-Phenicians, Arabs and Abyssinians; the Ural-Altaic consisting of Manchus, Mongols, Tartars including Turks and of Finns including Magyars; the Italic embracing the Greeks; the Teutonic including Anglo-Saxons; the Yankee-Anzac[2] and the Deutero-Slav.

Here are marked the successive waves of Aryan influence through Eurasia covering a period in inception far anterior to historical times and beginning concurrently with the crest of eastward Atlantean colonial civilization centered in Memphite Egypt, Sumerian Babylon, Minoan Troy, Dravidian India and Canaanite Palestine. The foundation emigration of Aryan root stock through northern Europe was followed by the initial outpourings of this new race in its first subdivision or the Indo-Iranic.

[1] Cf. Appendix D, p. 257.

[2] Yankee grew into renewed popularity as a substitute for the misnomer American during the 1914 European war which also brought into currency the corresponding term Anzac (Australian-New Zealand Army Corps) for Britishers of the antipodes.

Settlers in India conquered the Dravidians and to-day remain dominant in the peninsula. Through the highly evolved theosophic system of the Hindus a vast store of traditional occult knowledge has been preserved and given to the world in modern times. In a settlement further to the west the Persians long fought the succeeding subrace for rulership of the fertile crescent[1] and in the occultly all-important sixth century before Christ brought the first great Aryan stream to world supremacy under Cyrus.

Through the Iranians the public worship of the Great Central Flame was preserved while the Aryan Mysteries were spread and have been carried on until modern times under the external form of the Mithraic cult and the succeeding Manichean brother-hood. The independent pioneer spirit of the Aryans is to be found in a remnant of the original subrace still persisting in the shadow of old tribal form and known as Gipsies or Romanies.

The Semitic or second subrace was an emigrating stream of nomads which settled the central part of the fertile crescent and in the Arabian peninsula created a reservoir destined to send out the hardiest, bravest and most generous human stock of all Aryan specializations. The first Semite civilization was the Assyrian which battled with Egypt and eventually defeated her. Babylon and Jerusalem were con-quered by these tribesmen and under Semitic domi-nance they became the religious centers of the later

[1]A geographers' term for Mesopotamia, Syria and Palestine.

ancient world. Ezekiel who was an Aramean organized the formal solar cult and in Babylon fathered the Judaic priesthood which paved the way for Christ and also for the cabala and for the Middle-Age alchemists and the Rosicrucian order. The Arab family race[1] gave birth to modern occult philosophy and to profane science. Under the leadership of Mohammed these Saracens swept over most of the civilized world and so carried the culture impossible under a clouded Christianity. The organizing, consolidating and freely trading spirit of this race is shown today in the Jew who is its active worldwide representative.

The Ural-Altaic or third subrace swept into European prominence in early centuries of the Christian era through regular waves of Asiatic invasion. Genghis Khan was the mighty leader of this stream and Attila was the first great conqueror. The primal work of this differentiation was to bind Asia into a homogeneous mass unified sufficiently for the later Mars colonization. Through the Manchus it dominated China, through the Mongols India and through the Turks Islam. The Koreo-Japanese now are rising to supremacy in the far East while the Magyars in Europe until very recently have had through the Hungarian initiate lodge full charge and responsibility for the present general racial guidance upon the globe. By this wave racial intensity is particularized. The conscious cohesive tendency of

[1]For family race cf. p. 230.

selective association among humans which in eras to come will be very necessary in man's evolution is now particularly shown by the burning national spirit of the Magyars, Anatolian Turks and Japanese.

The Italic or fourth subrace first gained historical notice through the Hellenic branch of that mass of immigrants which crept down from the Aryan cradle in Asia to make its way along the Mediterranean. These drove back before them the peoples now surviving as Celts. Greeks, Romans, Italians, Spanish and French in order have been the disseminating agents of all focal culture of the great Aryan race. They have marked its central and numerically greatest point of activity. Their externalization of all form, beauty and activity in fullest creation of race bodies and of human experience and in widest latitude of individual expression is the work and accomplishment of a differentiation which has only just touched its maximum of usefulness.

The Teutonic or present dominant world race has taken the first step beyond the balance of cycle and as a substream it is marked by mental development and by that keen cold-blooded curiosity and skepticism noticeable in all modern critical effort. It includes the ordinary Anglo-Saxon type whether American or British and yet out of this English family is growing slowly a first suggestion of the sixth subrace which conveniently may be termed Yankee-Anzac since the square and long head with broad angular shoulders and lengthy arms and legs is the pro-

totype of the stock to come. Occult tradition states
that the new stream will develop in the beginnings of
Aryan cataclysm and that the seventh subrace will
follow the relatively imminent major world disasters
of the coming half millennium and will grow out of
the present Slavonic differentiation in the Atlantean
Accadian survivals.

The regular spokelike wave of these subraces
streaming out from the hub of the invisible Aryan
wheel clockwise[1] upon the face of Eurasia is plainly
noticeable up to the Teutonic present world domi-
nance. It will be equally evident in the actual growth
of the last two subraces and will result from a certain
amount of shift in the earth's axis necessary for the
continental adjustment to concurrent root race development.

Perfect orderliness is demonstrated not only in
the subraces but through their septenary division into
family races and even further in sevenfold constitution when finer attenuations are traced. The family
races may be taken through settled differentiation
marked by present language and national consciousness as in the Italic subrace or Greeks, Albanians,
Roumanians, Italians, French, Portuguese and Spanish and as in the Teutonic or Danes, Scandinavians,
Dutch, British, German, Swiss[2] and Anglo-Ameri-

[1]The whorl of Atlantean subrace emanation was counterclockwise.

[2]Racial overlapping is often very confusing as in the case of the
few Italians who belong to the Swiss Confederation and thereby
help develop the hexad consciousness in the pentad subrace but
who ethnically and linguistically have no relationship such as is

cans. They may be taken in a manner similar to the subraces through succession of supremacy and wave of influence now marked in the Teutonic series by two completed stages or the Germano-Barbarian and the Empire British and by a third just started in financial aggrandizement through the war of 1914 or the Anglo-American and formerly marked in the preceding Italic subrace by a complete and somewhat overlapping series or the Greek, Roman, Byzantine, Venetian-Genoese, Portuguese, Spanish and French.

Here is shown the development of present humanity by successive root, subroot and family race in direct relationship to the epochs and to the continents or terrestrial factor of occult philosophy.[1]

The second and a dual consideration in the threefold scheme of human manifestation is uncovered through the differentiation of race in relationship first to the planes and supersensual world domains and in relationship secondly to the racial consistency which reflects the development of the individual egos inhabiting race bodies.

So far the outline of races has dealt with the outer form in analysis of general progression in evolution of human type. First taken in cooperation with terrestrial condition the thread of this evolution must now be correlated with the planes.

more obvious in the French Swiss. This very confusion contributes importantly to the Swiss development.

[1]Study of the successions through the root races is difficult because of the thousands of millenia involved and therefore in this treatise the subordinate divisions have been employed for first definite illustration of the orderly and regular activity.

Here is the clue to interglobe block movements of human egos in the ship or ark of occult and ancient religious tradition. The Bible dramatizes the process through the story of Noah which except superficially and inaccurately is not concerned with the sinking of Atlantis but with the greater cataclysm of *akasic* record or the destruction of life on the moon[1] and transfer of a subordinate human and a complete animal stream from the heavenly body now the earth's satellite to Ararat or the present active planet created for the reception.

As the races succeed one another in a gradual specialization of form and a corresponding universalization of spirit dwelling within each body an obvious progress takes place in human manifestation. The persisting races which served their supremacy long ago in differentiative succession remain for analysis. The conventional teaching that bodies in these races are inhabited by laggard spirits is accurate only to a limited extent.

The negroes are remnants of the Lemurian root race and are to be classed with the now negroid survivors of the Rmoahals and Tlavatlis[2] or first two Atlantean subraces. These dark bodies serve for the incarnation of true human laggards of general

[1]The earth in prior incarnation. Cf. foot-note p. 223. The process which crystallized physical mass into the terrestrial globe upon its emergence from *pralaya* also crystallized matter about the astral effluvia of the prior incarnation and so led to the physical casting off of the visible moon as a placenta from which the molten earth emerged.

[2]The accepted names in occult philosophy but without dictionary recognition for either.

Lemurian-Atlantean type.[1] The forms are not used for new introduction of egos into the human kingdom but persist for backward egos.[2] Similarly the Indian tribes of the Americas are remnants of the Atlantean Toltec[3] or third subrace and are true laggards inhabiting forms which remain upon the globe for cooperation with the persisting Atlantean processes of evolution.[4]

[1]Complete definite classification of race-streams in their decadence is impossible. The identifications given in this treatise only call attention to racial type and to survival of definite human evolutionary tendency through the scheme of racial manifestation. All peoples in history intermingle to some extent while most differentiations of mankind undergo modification concurrent with their development. The black and brown peoples of the Interoceanic, African and West Indian groups invite correspondence to the characteristics of the emanative rays but the attempt after the lapse of nearly a million years since the first spread of the Rmoahals and Tlavatlis would be difficult while such a classification would be vitiated by the constant descent of laggards from half a dozen subsequent subraces into this dumping ground of present human evolution. (Cf. racial color, p. 247.) Classification would further be complicated by the presence in black races of some remnants of the sin-born of occult philosophy resulting from the early but no longer possible interbreeding of man and animal as represented particularly by the recently extinct Tasmanians and would be confused by a slight laggard descent of full human egos into animal form as found in the anthropoid apes which are the extreme of present life-stream degeneration.

[2]Not only as a reservoir of laggards who cannot get started upon a catching-up process but for those who seek and earn reentry into more virile stock. Graduation into later streams is achieved through miscegenation and resulting temporary hybrid cultures as in the striking American mulatto.

[3]The name of a mythical Mexican race and in occult philosophy the accepted term for the third race but without dictionary recognition as such.

[4]This red race in large colonies was able to survive the catastrophe which some ten thousand years ago covered the Americas with a blanket of volcanic ash and which snuffed out nearly all life

The four Atlantean subraces in following succession were great colonizing streams by comparison with that Rmoahal to Toltec development which largely took place on lands now beneath the ocean. The four later movements provided the differentiation further carried out in the present Aryan waves and so were sweeps of humanity eastward out over Africa and Eurasia.

The Poseidonian[1] subrace is best identified in the Hittites of history and monument. Through the Scythians at the beginning of our era and in the Armenians today this stream is preserved in its own

in the northern hemisphere. Navigation in both great oceans was cut off and a dread fear of the great deep was inculcated in all ancient peoples. The Toltec colonists were no longer hampered by the aggressive settlers of their own and succeeding subraces and were left free to roam a continent without molestation and to preserve thereon the several forms of primitive or cultured existence known to them. By the counterclockwise radiation of Atlantean streams this was a sphere suiting their growth. The Rmoahals and Tlavatlis were preserved only as a backwash after Atlantis sank. The backwash of the Toltecs survives in a combination with colonists coming around the globe from the west. Together these created the Interoceanic brown races of which generally the advancing Malayic blood might be called Toltec while the Polynesians or Australian type can be identified as remnants of the succeeding race now degenerating into the black reservoir. The Filipinos in the ethnology of occult philosophy are the oldest racial group which yet shows group advancement. By coordination they belong to this third Atlantean stream despite the admixture of bloods.

[1]Poseidon is the Grecian god of the sea who lends his name to that Atlantean island which met destruction through the black magic of this race. In popular occult teaching this substream is given the wholly meaningless designation of Original Turanian. Turan was the mythical ancestor of the Turk while Turanian is a designation which was once applied by conventional science to all non-Aryan and non-Semitic language of Asian origin and so is a term now abandoned as inexact and confusing.

laggard remnant.[1] A curiously pure survival of an earlier family race is found in the Basques. However it is not the survival of these particular Poseidonians that is of interest to the occult scientist since in evolution and supremacy the development belongs far back in the night of history and since the vast majority of egos particularly trained in that race body are to be found in the present Teutonic stream.[2] Rather as surviving in Palestine and through Canaanite blood the Poseidonians gave the Hebrew his features and that differentiation of Semite characteristic which has made the Jew of value in the world. Three thousand years ago the Hittites through development of iron and in the training of horses opened the way for the present epoch of non-magical and material world dominion. These things and not the Armenian or Basque shred of race are first considerations of occult study.

The Sabians[3] or fifth Atlantean development is interesting through a direct survival in the Berbers and Copts and because it is also to be identified through a first still-persisting subordinate cycle of

[1] For the Poseidonian Polynesian backwash cf. foot-note[4] p. 233.

[2] Similarly the Italic subrace is largely developing Toltec egos coincident with the civilization of the Indians and their interbreeding with other races which is particularly prevalent in South America. The Yankee-Anzac development meanwhile is cooperating with fifth Atlantean subrace remnants. Cf. foot-note[5] p. 236.

[3] The Sabians were the star worshipers of mysterious origin in Syria and they provide a convenient name for this stream. The confusing term Original Semite in popular occultism had its inception in the fact that a migration of Sabians provided the Aryan root stock. This race far antedates any Semitic development and such a designation is inept.

evolution among subrace survivors or in the Celts.[1]
Again is found the curious pure survival of an earlier
family race[2] in the Letts.   The Sabians were the Atlantean differentiation from which the first physical
Aryan stock was developed by emigration in response
to a geometrical necessity for building a fifth root
race out of a fifth subrace.[3]   In the Teutonic fifth
subrace of the existing Aryan root is completed the
five recapitulation and for the development of the
sixth Aryan subrace preparatory to an eventual birth
of the Aquarian sixth root stock it is necessary that
a stimulation of the five element occur in the six.[4]
This is brought about by the Celtic softening of
Teutonic blood in both Britain and Anglo-America.[5]

The Sabians were the most brilliant Atlantean
stream.   They built pyramids and temples and left
the impress of their civilization not only upon Egypt
and in Sumerian Babylon but throughout the world
from Yucatan where the Mayas are a present cor-
rupt remnant in Indian blood to Asia and its buried
Aryan sacred city in the Gobi desert and to central
Africa with its mines of ancient red gold.   Their
worldwide spiritual domination of the human life

[1] The seventh family race. Cf. foot-note[3] p. 179.
[2] The sixth.
[3] In other words a smaller and a larger cycle coincide at the
point of corresponding differentiation. The races do not so much
succeed each other as they express progressive stages of development. Their constant overlapping is help rather than hindrance to
their progress.
[4] To induce the monad which later projects the emanation of a
root stock.
[5] Specially marked by Welsh influence in Britain and by the large
initial Irish emigration to the United States.

stream exercised from the Egyptian lodge was ceded by them directly to the Ural-Altaic subrace of the present Aryan wave where the responsibility must remain until the end of the epoch.[1]

The Accadian[2] or sixth great Atlantean race is revealed in a flashing splendor of art and science and through a real commercial genius shown by the Phenicians of history who were mixed survivors of the vast Aegean civilization set up from the isle of Crete by a family race Accadian colonization. Cnossus, Troy and Sidon were among the great city-communities which long preserved in the smaller group the Accadian or sixth-power extreme individuality to be noted in each personality of the present Yankee-Anzac advance types. This race through the medium of the first Greeks yielded its colonizing and disseminating function to the present Italic differentiation which through Hellenic, Roman and

[1]This is the Rosicrucian sixteen-races idea which fundamentally is associated with the spiritual responsibility cycle. The Lemurian differentiation only became a true race in its seventh substream while the Aquarian will not remain a manifestation of man with racial distinction except through its first subordinate differentiation. The Atlantean and Aryan each with seven subraces complete the sixteen total. The tutelary initiate lodge belongs to the seventh nameless branch of the third race, the fifth or Sabian of the fourth, the third or Ural-Altaic of the fifth and the first or un-named branch of the coming Aquarian. Here is an inverse numerical influence of the decad or the seven and three added, ennead or the five and four, octad or the three and five and heptad or the one and six. These display the Pythagorean initiation quaternary. Cf. p 252. For sixteen cf. foot-note[3] p. 128.

[2]The conventional term in occult philosophy and again a misnomer but at least a name pre-Semite. Accad was the southernmost of two kingdoms which were merged into Babylonia at the dawn of history.

Spanish influences in particular spread the Aryan root stock throughout the globe.

The laggard egos are particularly to be found in the actual Accadian Dravidians of India and in some few scattered related groups. The still virile race expression is through the final Accadian or Slavonic races.[1] A curiously pure survival of the ancient Accadian art and crafts has been transmitted from the Aegean civilization into the modern Bohemian or Czech.[2] While the process lies far in the future the Accadian-Slavonic seventh family race already shows the development which will create out of it the seventh Aryan subrace to succeed the Yankee-Anzac in world dominance. It will be enough akin to the present Russian people to be termed for convenience the Deutero-Slav.

The Mongolian or seventh Atlantean race like all opening or closing epochal specializations was originally and relatively a small group. No true lag-

[1]The Czechs and Poles are the principal offspring of the sixth family race while the southern and eastern Slavonic differentiations constitute the final family group of the Accadians. The first of these two races has passed its crest but Russia will probably reach a supremacy towards the close of the present century.

[2]These pure centers of survival as the Toltec Red Indians, the Poseidonian Basques, the Sabian Letts and through their art the Accadian Czechs are illustration of the principle of visible focal establishments that permit a race to function. (Cf. p. 124.) A race differs little from an invisible brotherhood or a tangible community. Sodom and Gomorrah would have escaped destruction had ten righteous people remained in either place to act as this nucleus in form for the invisible cosmic pattern of the evolutionary process. (Cf. Gen. 18; 32.) The Theosophical Society was formed in 1875 for this reason and to be such a nucleus and it so served during critical years of spiritual necessity. (Cf. foot-note p. 242.)

gards are to be found since the race itself is the final sweep in divine economy. It consists of a development close enough to spiritual structural simplicity to allow it to provide evolution for all egos unable to advance through preceding differentiations.[1] In every epoch until the last of each planetary cycle the seventh subrace serves to catch and carry laggards. Few egos are left behind by any life-stream.

This subrace further permits the development into human state of sufficiently individualized animal egos. Through this experience and after an initial incarnation these egos may gravitate to the differentiation that has attracted them into a higher life-stream. Of these egos the ones who cannot adjust themselves to human consciousness are unable to return to animal state and so constitute the groups that alone can be termed Mongolian laggards. These are the Asiac-Hyperboreans and the American Arctic tribes.[2]

Relatively few of the Mongolians are egos belonging to the earth's human life-stream. In addition to the groups outlined and some guiding spirits that cannot outwardly be identified in the Ural-Altaic controlling subrace to which they belong the

[1] Thus all races in the present epoch except the frankly laggard blacks and the clearly advancing Caucasians display Asiatic characteristics. Even the red men show an apparent ethnic relationship to the Mongolian stream while the Mongolian idiot is born to families Aryan in all lines for generations.

[2] Who by the attraction of affinity dwell upon the remains of the first and second continents.

yellow peoples who constitute a very appreciable proportion of the earth's population are human colonists from the planet Mars.[1]   Physiologically but superficially these are to be identified by the socket structure of the eyes and the characteristic fold of the upper lid rather than a slant not uncommon in other races.   No outward sign is reliable since the body type is loaned by the earth's own stream and has included to a now rapidly decreasing degree the egos of workers and helpers in this class.[2]   Thus in China the Ural-Altaic Manchus have been forced to yield control to the Mongolian Chinese while in Japan the Aryan blood is rapidly diminishing and that race is becoming Mongolian rather than Ural-Altaic through subtraction on higher planes.[3]

Material evolution on the planet Mars is slightly

[1]The interchange of human streams from planet to planet. Cf. p. 99.   Note that this is the type of occult information which suffers particularly at the hands of literalists.   Lifted from its context the Mars teaching would seem childish or at the best foolish and so hitherto has been held a mystery.   Indeed interplanetary cooperation can only properly be understood through analogy.   Thus a young boy must borrow the intelligence and understanding of his parents, teachers and elder playmates.   Only at adultship does he leave the house of his youth to become an individual and this departure from the parental home may be a figurative if not a literal fact.   That intelligence and thought forms are here loaned rather than physical vehicles is only the difference between the individual and life-stream spheres or between the interchanges within the limitation of physical and astral worlds respectively.

[2]Many of these voluntarily will go to Mars to aid general evolution in the manner that Lords of Venus served nascent humanity upon the earth in early epochs.

[3]Aided by miscegenation and by colonization of Japanese in countries where they are sufficiently unwelcome to create in any Aryan individual a wish to draw out of the Mongolian form.

behind progress upon the earth. From a Mars perspective the egos of its humanity have here a shadow consciousness in introduction to human form.[1] The interpretation on that planet would state this to be an occurence in that higher plane which any sunward planet is to its physical neighbor.[2] On that sphere itself a lower form of mineral constitution and vegetable activity[3] is evolving in preparation for the receipt in a new round of its human life-stream which upon arrival will immediately call into physical expression the always correlating animal manifestation that now on Mars is a brooding cosmic warmth.

From the earth point of view the presence of visiting Mars life balances and permits the presence here of the large colonization upon invisible planes of egos not exactly akin to the terrestrial human stage but belonging to the humanity of the planet Venus and brought by the initiates of that life stream to maintain their own being and power while here domiciled.[4]

Occult philosophy has known for some years that the tutelary function of the earth brotherhoods has been ceded temporarily to these elder spirits of the wave formerly resident upon the globe. This author-

[1]Thus not really present as humans in the Mars human life-stream but literally earth-stream entities and so no exception to a principle in fact. Cf. p. 91.

[2]The occult geometrical fact behind the Sinnett error in the curious Theosophical Mars-Mercury controversy.

[3]An etheric quickening preparatory to the specialization of a heavier life-supporting atmosphere. Cf. foot-note[3] p. 99.

[4]Cf. pp. 99, 133.

ity[1] must remain in force until the cataclysm that will usher in the Aquarian epoch. Man as an individual will obtain more power through a destruction of democracy now imminent but the individual will not again be a ruler until the crest of Yankee-Anzac subrace supremacy and after a period of widespread destruction during which both the Mars and Venus streams will leave the globe. From the earth point of view the principal purpose served by the Mars-Mongolians upon the globe is to provide the opposing force to humanity in a warfare which necessarily must be bitter, vicious and protracted enough to result in the destruction of an age and in the inauguration of a new epoch.[2]

In any fourth cyclic planetary position the fifth epoch or first one beyond quaternary recapitulation is always most critical throughout physical realms.

[1]Invoked by the hierophant of the Hungarian Lodge and not imposed from higher realms. A previous reinforcement of the Ural-Altaic brothers in the present crisis followed the request for help to the Eastern lodge when the Rosicrucian weakness became apparent in 1861. Cf. foot-note[2] p. 141.

[2]This is not prophecy in the sense of prediction but is analysis of tendency through a dramatization of cosmic process. A case in point is Tolstoy's famous prophecy of the ominous figure who would come out of the north to overrun Europe until 1925. The growth of the necessary political and military machine was noticeable in Russia while a great leader rose to prominence and could be recognized easily as an initiate member of one of the brotherhoods incarnate in a clouded personality for the purpose of the task to which he had volunteered. As prophecy Tolstoy's vision was accurate but not as prediction. Humanity racing towards destruction in abuse of liberties which it had earned through centuries finally permitted itself to be slowed sufficiently to obviate the necessity for the movement out of the north. The movement therefore never started. Cf. p. 6. *Verbum sat sapienti.*

Only once in each complete scheme of human manifestation is this triad of interplanetary cooperation to be identified through an objective humanity. For that reason the end of the present particular epoch is known universally in prophecy as Armageddon[1] or the cosmic parallel to a terrible battle fought to achieve the material balance in human evolution to spirituality both for the individual and the race.

Objective major interplanetary cooperation reflects a lesser exchange of influences from plane to plane and this constitutes a recapitulation which is regular and eternally significant. The laggard remnants of Atlantean and Lemurian races are now neither Atlantean nor Lemurian but rather a present process in life-stream activity may here be identified with Atlantis and with its epoch as well as the dominant Atlantean race survivors.[2]

The Aryan is a physical manifestation while in accurate description the Atlantean may be said to have been etheric. The actual and gradual shading of cosmic mass from original non-matter to physical substance[3] is never indicated by sharp demarcation in the lower atoms themselves despite the fact that their unfolding must be understood through a dimensional distinction. The divine guidance of human

[1]In geography the plain of Esdraelon that lies between Jerusalem which is symbol of the higher responsible nature and Galilee which is a lower irresponsible counterpart in these physiological signatures of the Holy Land.

[2]Cf. p. 231. Here is a second division in the second consideration of this threefold analysis through human manifestation.

[3]Visually illustrated in mediumistic materializations.

evolution entrusted to the Ural-Altaic subrace is a literal control of the Mongolian or principal Atlantean and Mars humanities and has been a complete and is now a subordinate spiritual suzerainty of the world through the nature brotherhood centered objectively among the Magyars and known to the western world as the Rosicrucians.[1] The traditional teachings of this brotherhood have centered in alchemy or a transmutation of essences which becomes etheric control of chemical matter and have concerned themselves with the nature spirits or gnomes, sylphs, undines and salamanders. The modern and public Rosicrucian instruction is frankly concentrated upon etheric development through the fluidic double or vital vehicle of man.

Similarly Lemurian activity was astral and still remains so. As the Atlantean or fourth stage dealt and continues to deal with man so the third or Lemurian activity has been and remains animal. In the actual third root race humanity was no more than animal in intelligence and structure. Man was guided by the great hierarchy of workers which in modern times is unkindly termed the Black Brotherhood and is sometimes known as the Manichean[2] order. Animals themselves are only evil or vicious

[1]Rosicrucian throughout this treatise has no particular reference to any established and organized group either upon visible or invisible planes. The Hungarian Lodge is a symbol and a focal spiritual urge but not itself an institution. Cf. foot-notes pp. 59[2], 200[2].

[2]Cf. p. 227. The designation Manichean like the term Rosicrucian has no reference to tangible organization and none such exists.

when driven into artificial conditions and these present-day Lemurian forces for all the occasional surface voodoism and alleged black magic are nevertheless constructive and working for the general evolution of the life-stream through elementals which are not to be confounded with the nature spirits but are rather the astral intelligences created, strengthened and destroyed by the consciousness activities of the two higher kingdoms.

Hyperborean activity originally was lunar and therefore it remains upon its upper astral plane. Mankind in this epoch entered the plant stage.[1] The Pandean[2] brotherhood is superior in responsibility to the Manicheans in the sense that this group of workers is exalted above the Rosicrucians. It is concerned objectively with the vegetable kingdom and is responsible for that consciousness of the globe itself which lies in the second kingdom and which carries awareness in the second great cosmic world. Through this brotherhood the Venus initiates and their attendants are to be identified upon return to the earth.[3]

In the Polarian epoch man was objectively undifferentiated. Each ego was merely a vortex of force

[1]Cf. pudding-bags, foot-note p. 94.

[2]The god Pan was the ancient spirit given general tutelary dignity over all pure nature forces and so associated with the simple globe consciousness. He was said in ancient tradition to die upon the cessation of the oracles and he has given his name to the general life-stream of the present Venus humanity and to the principal continent last occupied by them on this globe.

[3]Etheric initiate development on Venus corresponds to activity upon the lunar plane in the earth sphere. Cf. foot-note[3] p. 128.

recapitulating its individual Saturn period and so hardly to be described in terms of the tangible. No Polarian brotherhood exists but the higher conscious-ness of the earth spirit itself is rather to be identi-fied with the mineral kingdom.[1]   Similarly no cos-mic brotherhoods exist to be correlated with the Aryan, Aquarian or Hepatogenic epochs.   Through these man himself by initiation takes on the various responsible functions of life processes about him and so relieves workers of superior life-streams by per-mitting them to return to their own evolution in spheres where they are human and free to grow as individuals.[2]

The Atlantean was the balance epoch of fourth position with no mystery schools open to general humanity.   In the Aryan initiations candidates are trained to relieve workers with the animal kingdom or with the emotional nature in man and so these assist the Black Brotherhood.   Therefore the first association of initiates out of the human stream for identification is called by contrast the White Lodge. Achievement of white mastership demands perfect conquest of the animal nature.

In the Aquarian epoch the human adepts will re-lieve the Pandean workers and as brothers of the flame will form the Golden Lodge.   In this same epoch will take place a subordinate development in which the present animal life-stream on Venus will

[1] The complete embracing arc of manifestation. Cf. the reflection of the divine fire plane in the lower physical, foot-note[3] p. 128.
[2] Cf. foot-note[2] p. 240.

provide an order or brotherhood of egos then human in a pre-Adamite stage for relief of the Rosicrucian workers with the nature spirits on the earth.[1]

The third consideration of mankind's manifestation through the races is provided in color.[2]

In occult philosophy racial color[3] is the mark of the individual's dimension by evolutionary consistency. It is both indication of his individualization through involutionary emphasis and key to his universal cohesiveness or coagulation into larger supersensual spheres by evolution. White is the summarizing color and through contrast with white the other racial hues are judged. The dominant hierarchy objectively or subjectively is always white and by the traditions of several ancient peoples the great visible god from over the sea was so described.[4] In Lemuria the dominant subrace was approximately white rather than dark and so in Atlantis and throughout Aryan distribution of races.

[1]The puzzling marriage of the philosophers or humanized principle to the nature spirits in the Rosicrucian teachings is the provision for first spiritual intelligence in lower form by sacrifice or by a sacrament involving conscious communion of spirit with the flesh or physical being. In all occult legends of man's origin the higher intelligences first refused to give themselves in this fashion and thereby held back cosmic evolution. In the ancient temples the priests as part of their duties served young women who wished to pass from virginity to recognized adultship and this ceremony for all its proper repugnance to modern conceptions and all its staggering immorality in decadent mysteries was yet originally a pure sacrament given in understanding. Cf. matrimony, p. 250.

[2]A universal error is the assumption that color is constant with race and that hue is the basic identification of human root stock.

[3]Cf. Appendix D, p. 257.

[4]The Quetzalcoatl and allied myths of Mexico and Central America.

Yellow is the focal or central color. It shades to red or ruddy, to brown or the representation of purple and to black or the degeneracy of green through its deeper olive. From yellow the races reach upward toward the ideal through pallid or the representation of blue and through golden or radiant which as a primary tint is orange. White is the seventh or divine summary out of which the other colors emanate.

This is the full scheme of human manifestation in focus through three separate but cooperative processes of succession in stages.

INITIATION AND THE SACRAMENTS

Initiation is the extension of consciousness through growth deliberately induced and is evolution through but in advance of environment.[1]

Except in organized objective occult schools it is not a process to be measured by exact rules or set achievement of result. Even the membership and make-up of the great brotherhoods is not static but rather identifies conveniently the functions and responsibilities on higher planes. A Rosicrucian worker today must be found tomorrow in a Manichean group or again performing some task in seclusion without associates or identifiable affiliation. The White Lodge is no more than a general term for souls of a given development perhaps drawn together actually by affinity of purpose and unity of

[1] Cf. p. 201 and penance p. 251.

desire but wholly unorganized in any sense humanly cognizable.[1]

Initiation is in response to divine rather than human law and so it is commonly symbolized by the ennead or nine and the sacred tetrad or four. Yet it is truly septenary despite its traditional nine lesser and four greater degrees. The lesser group are no more than the triad of activity in recapitulation of each three through the others. The four superimposed upon this triangle gives the heptad of the original mysteries. Except in conventional representation the lesser and greater are undergone concurrently.

In occult philosophy a rather technical distinction exists between terms.[2] An initiate is one who has developed supernormal faculties and knowledge of the higher planes in conscious association with the brotherhoods. A brother is one who has developed to the point of continuous human existence[3] between lives and who consciously or unconsciously serves the brotherhoods in incarnation. An adept is one whose abnormal development involves superphysical or magical power and he may or may not be either an initiate or brother but usually is both. A master is a brother or initiate with an adept's powers and is one who possesses direct brotherhood commission and cooperation.

[1]Cf. p. 121 ff.

[2]Seldom recognized in popular expositions and therefore involved in much confusion. These distinctions have no dictionary authority.

[3]Cf. p. 124.

Initiation has been recognized by all world religions and until very recent times was commonly understood in the Christian church. In the ritual it is represented by the sacraments which in turn are further interpreted by the traditional deadly sins and chief virtues.[1] All life explains initiation while the sacraments interpret life.

Matrimony is the sacrament of the element of flesh and therefore represents the ability of the initiate truly to enter into any experience for the help of humanity no matter how gross it seemingly may be. The sin is covetousness or desire for something without understanding in experience. The virtue is faith.

Eucharist is the sacrament of the element of blood through which the initiate partakes of the life in all matter.[2] The occult understanding is that the eucharist consists not in acceptance of the nature of the Christ spirit but in receptivity just for the instant sufficient to permit contact so that by reversal[3] the initiate may add and pour individual consciousness into the cosmic ego's spiritual being. The sin is lust or acceptance of ecstasy solely for the self-joy of it. The virtue is chastity.

Unction or the sacrament through oil symbolizes the healing functions of the initiate. The sin is gluttony or that first consideration of self which as a subtle seed grows into animal appetite. The virtue

[1]Cf. Appendix C, p. 256.
[2]Cf. p. 138.
[3]The power of the ennead or Pythagorean nine. Cf. p. 253.

is that all-embracing tolerance traditionally expressed as temperance or the understanding of a point of view foreign to the self.

Penance is the sacrament of earth whereby the initiate lowers his own nature in humble realization of a capacity for downward growth akin to his development in any heavenward direction.[1] The sin is anger or misuse of the divine fire within. The virtue is fortitude.

Baptism or the sacrament of water represents the growth of the initiate into true cosmic understanding. The sin is envy or surrender to the inner fears of the self. The virtue is hope.

Confirmation or the fire sacrament is for the initiate his constant rebirth into the divine. The sin is sloth or idle withdrawing from the world. The virtue is prudence.

Ordination is the sacrament of air and accompanies the wisdom received once by the initiate and once by him given to his successor.[2] The sin is the

[1] In the final initiation this is the descent into Hell recorded of Christ after Calvary and is the completion in the individual of the full manifest arc of humanity. Cf. foot-note[1] p. 246 and p. 200.

[2] This is a recurrent process at each stage of initiation and is the cosmic principle behind the fact that information may be given through the veil only once in an epoch whether the recipient uses or abuses it. It is also the deeper principle involved in the correlative obligation upon the initiate always to hold some part of his knowledge secret and inviolate until it is replaced by higher knowledge. In this latter necessity the familiar focal establishment becomes here a center of superphysical knowledge. (Cf. foot-note p. 125.) Whatever this particular understanding the initiate must have a successor prepared and must transmit it to him immediately before death to avoid an awkward and sometimes dangerous *karmic* link to physical manifestation.

most dangerous of all or pride. The virtue is a true poised sympathy within or charity.

THE HEPTAD AND ITS PROPHET

The heptad is manifestation. Occult focus always is septenary and so is the guide to all objective analysis.

General and scientific understanding of the permanent and intricate relationship involved in manifestation is due not to conventional occult philosophy but to the great prophet of the heptad or the German scholar whose work gave birth to critical philosophy. Immanuel Kant was a thinker who never traveled more than forty miles away from his birthplace but who nevertheless successfully focused his mind upon the universe. By his own efforts and laboring alone he unwittingly taught modern intelligence the occult principle that truth is only to be gained through the medium of sensual contact and objective result.

THE FOUR REMAINING SCHOOLS

The school of the heptad or seven is the Illuminati or the unorganized association in earth life of the illuminated while upon invisible planes it is the great White Lodge. Here is development of knowledge by the simple induction of enlarged consciousness.

The school of the octad or eight is the Ecstatic. This and the two remaining are open only to initiates though in ages past man through the phallic rites of the temples was permitted a measure of participation in this school in order to increase his individuality by a deeper plunge into experience.[1]

The school of the ennead or nine is the Creative and of the decad or ten the Prophetic. These deal respectively with operative white magic which occasionally is found upon the left hand or in destructive aspect and with the regular incarnation of the brothers for definite service through racial embodiment in smaller cycles as well as through great cosmic solar avatars.

[1]Some remnants of this method exist in a modern world where their presence objectively is dangerous and retrogressive. Cf. p. 21.

THE OCTONARY CONSTITUTION OF SPACE

Dimension		Recapitulation		Kingdom	Planetary and Pythagorean Aspects		
					Activity	Response	Limitation
0	Point	Logos	♄ Thrones	Chaos		☽ Inertia	☿ Motion
1	Line	Planetary Spirits	♃ Dominions	Mineral	☽ Inertia	☿ Motion	♀ Growth
2	Plane	Nature Spirits	♂ Virtues	Vegetable	☿ Motion	♀ Growth	☉ Being
3	Solid	Human Spirits	☉ Powers	Animal	♀ Growth	☉ Being	♂ Form
4	Sphere	Atom		Human	☉ Being	♂ Form	♃ Space
5	Planet	Individual	☽ Angels	Nature Spirits	♂ Form	♃ Space	♄ Duration
6	Solar System	Race	☿ Archangels	Planetary Spirits	♃ Space	♄ Duration	♅ Manifestation
7	Cosmos	Life-Stream	♀ Principalities	Logos	♄ Duration	♅ Manifestation	♆ Creation

☽Moon, ☿Mercury, ♀Venus, ☉Sun, ♂Mars, ♃Jupiter, ♄Saturn, ♅Uranus, ♆Neptune.

THE OCTONARY SCHEME OF WORLDS AND MAN

WORLDS	PLANES	THE VEHICLES OF MAN			
		THEOSOPHICAL		ROSICRUCIAN	
		Sinnett[1]	Besant[2]	Heindel[5]	Steiner[7]
PHYSICAL { Physical-Universe	Physical	*Rupa* Body	*Sthula-Sarira* Dense body	Dense body	Physical body
	Etheric	*Prana-Jiva* Vitality	*Linga Sarira* Etheric double	Vital body	Etheric or Vital body
ASTRAL { Lunar Ocean	Astral	*Linga Sarira* Astral body	*Prana*[3]	Desire body	Astral or Soul body
	Lunar	*Kama rupa* Animal soul	Animal soul / Astral body[4]	Mind[6]	Sentient soul[8]
MENTAL { Cosmic Ocean	Mental	*Manas* Human soul	Mental body	Human Spirit	Ego or Rational soul[9]
	Solar		Causal body		Spirit-self[10] (*Manas*)
SPIRIT { Cosmic Fire	Spirit	*Buddhi* or Spiritual body / Buddhic body		Life Spirit	Life Spirit (*Buddhi*)
	Fire	*Atma* or Spirit		Divine Spirit	Spirit-Man (*Atma*)

[1]*Esoteric Buddhism*, A. P. Sinnett, 1884; classification accepted in *The Key to Theosophy*, H. P. Blavatsky, 1889, and in *The Ocean of Theosophy*, Wm. Q. Judge, 1893. [2]*The Ancient Wisdom*, Annie Besant, 1897. [3]Considered by Mrs. Besant to be the life force of the physical plane and not one of man's principles. [4]Also given as *kama*. [5]*The Rosicrucian Cosmo-Conception*, Max Heindel, 1909. [6]Considered by Mr. Heindel to lie in the lower or concrete thought half of the following or mental world. [7]*Outline of Occult Science*, Rudolf Steiner, 1909, authorized translation. [8]Considered by Mr. Steiner an integral part of the soul body and not one of the principles of man. [9]Also given as intellectual soul. [10]Also given as consciousness soul.

THE SEVEN GREAT KEYS AND SACRAMENTS

THE KEY TO KNOWLEDGE	DEPARTMENT IN OCCULT PHILOSOPHY	Planetary Coordinate	SACRAMENT AND ELEMENT	DEADLY SIN AND CHIEF VIRTUE
Microcosmic or Solar	Laws of Force Initiation	Saturn	Ordination Air	Pride Charity
Biological or History	Laws of Process Cycles	Jupiter	Confirmation Fire	Sloth Prudence
Macrocosmic or Lunar	Laws of Dimension The Zodiac	Mars	Baptism Water	Envy Hope
Musical or Vibration	Laws of Geometry Relationship	Sun	Penance Earth	Anger Fortitude
Chemical or Transmutation	Laws of Phenomena Objectivity	Venus	Unction Oil	Gluttony Temperance
Phallic or Ecstasy	Laws of Divination Correspondence	Mercury	Eucharist Blood	Lust Chastity
Physiological or Function	Laws of Development Consciousness	Moon	Matrimony Flesh	Covetousness Faith

THE SEPTENARY DIFFERENTIATION OF PROCESS

THE STATES			THE SUCCESSIONS			
	Space[2]	Consciousness[3]	Planetary[7]	Epochal[8]	Racial[9]	Individual
Matter	Space[2]	Consciousness[3]	Planetary[7]	Epochal[8]	Racial[9]	Individual
Etheric[1]	Solvent	Saturn	Saturn	Polarian	Indo-Iranic	Black[10]
Gaseous	Precipitate	Janus[4]	Jupiter	Hyperborean	Semitic	Brown[11]
Liquid	Sublimate	Diana[5]	Mars	Lemurian	Ural-Altaic	Red
Solid	Carbon	Tellus[6]	Sun	Atlantean	Italic	Yellow
Alcoholic	Resolvent	Jupiter	Venus	Aryan	Teutonic	Pallid[12]
Spirituous	Catalytic	Venus	Mercury	Aquarian	Yankee-Anzac	Golden[13]
Rapt	Metabolic	Vulcan	Moon	Hepatogenic	Deutero-Slav	White

[1]Fourth of Crookes. [2]Planetary chemical natures. [3]Theosophical chains and by recapitulation rounds, Rosicrucian periods and by recapitulation revolutions. [4]Sun. [5]Moon. [6]Earth with Mars and Mercury halves. [7]Chaldean order. [8]Root races, continents and epochs. [9]Subraces of the fifth or Aryan root. [10]Occultly olive or green. [11]Purple. [12]Blue. [13]Orange.

INDEX

Aberration 116,193
Abnormality 54,128,131,136,186
Abrams 32
Absolute 59,91,144,145,153,167,178, 182,187,206
Abstract SEE form, mental
Abstruseness 53,150,176,222
Abyssinian 226
Accadian 230,237,238
Acids 94,199
Activity (SEE ALSO chemistry) 52,55, 56,61,65,68,69,71,82,85,87,92,93,94, 95,96,97,103,105,108,109,112,114, 117,127,128,130,132,134,135,137,138, 140,144,145,152,154,158,164,165,166, 167,170,172,173,174,175,176,184,185, 186,190,192,196,202,203,207,215,254
Adam 112,169,247
Adept SEE initiation
Adjustment 192ff,226
Adrenals 195
Adultship 158,247
Aegean 237,238
Affinity 170,184,248
Affirmation 187
African 211,233,234,236
Age SEE epoch, experience, geology, time
Age, Aquarian 212
Age, Golden 200,205
Age, Piscian 212
Air (SEE ALSO atmosphere) 203,251, 256
Akasa (SEE ALSO tradition) 38,223, 232
Albanian 230
Alchemy 33,113,160,213,228,244
Alcoholic 83,213,257
Alimentary-urogenital 168
Allotropic 102
Altaic SEE Ural-Altaic
Alternation 50,51,112,169,177
Altruism 124,132
America (SEE ALSO Indian, United States, Yankee) 74,211,212,233,235, 236,239,247
Analogy 124,201
Analysis 10,52,58,111,135,220ff,252
Anatomy 185,195
Ancient Wisdom, The 255
Angels 92,201,254

Anger 88,251,256
Angle (SEE ALSO horoscopy) 78
Anglo-Saxon (SEE ALSO English, Yankee) 226,229
Animal 35,50,71,72,80,88,91,93,94, 102,104,105,110,112,116,118,123,131, 137,150,158,159,162,163,198,199,201, 206,207,232,233,239,244,245,246,250, 254
Anthropoids 88,89,233
Anthropology 70,74,216,224ff
Ants 99
Anzac 226,235,237,238,242,257
Apana 169
Apes 88,89,233
Aphasia 41,51
Apocalypse 106,107,119
Appendix 88,212
Appetite 84,169,172,192,195,250
Aquarian 212,222,236,237,242,246,257
Aquarius 12,212
Arabian 27,65,160,226,227,228
Aramean 226,228
Ararat 232
Arc (SEE ALSO horoscopy) 68,206,208, 209,220,246,251
Archangels 201,254
Archeology 24,187
Archetypes SEE pattern, form
Arctic 239
Aries 12,165,173
Ark 232
Armageddon 131,243
Armenian 234,235
Articulation 91,107,168
Art 12,132,237,238
Aryan 96,142,179,185,211,223,226, 227,230,234,236,237,238,239,240,243, 246,247,257
Asia (SEE ALSO Eurasia) 228,229,234, 236,239
Aspect (SEE ALSO concepts, horoscopy) 70,81,94,139,170,254
Aspiration 133,139
Association 123,124,125,128,138,151, 153,159,174,182,200
Assyrian 226,227
Astral (SEE ALSO spiritism, tradition, vehicle) 16,83,118,119,120,122,125, 128,146,147,148,163,168,197,206,223, 232,244,245

258

Astral plane 128,130,145,209,223,255
Astral world 128,130,131,132,201,207, 223,240,255
Astrology (SEE ALSO fortune-tellers, horoscopy) 33,49,52,55,63,65,67,70, 74,76,83,108,115,133,141,142,165, 173,179,204,205,212,213,220,222,257
Astronomy 67,193
Atavism 193
Atlantean 73,99,211,224,225,226,230, 232,233,234,235,236,237,238,243,244, 246,247,257
Atlantic 211
Atmosphere 102,241
Atom (SEE ALSO seed-atom) 63,66,69, 92,95,97,101,123,125,126,145,147, 150,151,152,166,194,212,243,254
Atomic weight 223
Atonement 26,85,117,138,139,182,194
Atrophy 195,196
Attenuation 52,57,75,108,147,148,153, 172,199,230
Attila 228
Attraction 65,101
Aura 68,104,106,109,157,168
Australian 88,89,226,234
Authority 4,8,189,191,241
Avatars 182,253
Axiom, Hermetic 32,63

Babylonian 142,221,226,227,228,236, 237
Bacon 12,190
Bags, pudding 94,245
Bahaism 31
Balance (SEE ALSO equilibrium) 87,89, 90,109,110,112,140,154,167
Banana 99
Baptism 251,256
Basques 235,238
Beauty 12,229
Bees 99
Beginning SEE differentiation, genesis
Being 61,62,68,95,96,103,105,109,116, 117,118,125,126,127,134,139,140, 144ff.160,167,168,169,170,173,175, 177,178,180,182,184,187,188,192,193, 196,202,203,210,215,217,219,220,221, 254
Benediction 95
Benjamine 31
Berbers 235
Besant 255
Bible 24,33,46,64,95,103,189,224,232
Bigotry 10,107
Biology 50,74,105,183,215
Birth 157,159,182,206,207
Black (SEE ALSO brotherhoods, spirit-ism) 233,239,244,248,253,257
Blavatsky 12,70,166,208,255
Blood 110,139,169,211,250,256

Blue 248,257
Blush 88
Bodies, heavenly 103,129,131,148,165
Body (SEE ALSO Christ, vehicle) 185, 194,196,206
Bohemian 238
Bone 109,196
Books 12,50,197,208
Botany 50,56,58
Brahma 46,98,204
Brain (SEE ALSO mental, mind) 57, 106,155
Breath 88,107
Breaths, solar 169
British SEE English
Brotherhood (SEE ALSO humanitarian) 96,124,126,138
Brotherhoods (SEE ALSO hierarchies, ini-tiate, initiation) 38,124,125,126,141, 185,188,200,227,228,237,238,241,242, 244,245,246,247,248,249
Brown 233,234,248,257
Buddhism 26,31,208
Buddhism, Esoteric 255
Byzantium 231

Cabala 27,106,113,228
Calendar 40
California 212
Calvary 138,152,251
Calvin 24
Canals, semicircular 168
Canaanite 226,235
Canons 178,189
Carbon 71,102,173,213,257
Cardiac 107,173
Cassava 199
Cataclysm 50,73,98,100,137,142,211, 224,230,232,233,242
Catalysis 83,168,213,257
Caucasian (SEE ALSO white) 239
Cause, first SEE emanation
Cell SEE embryology, sphere
Cells 63,66,68,110,169,193,196,198
Celt 229,236
Center 62,66,67,68,69,76,84,85,125, 126,144,149,151,153,163,182,219,222, 238,251
Centers, somatic 75,83,105,109,112, 159,163,165,170,195,227
Central America 247
Cerebral 173
Ceremonies SEE rites, sacrament
Cessation 136,137,245
Chains 204,208,213,257
Chaldean 133,220,222,257
Chalice 106
Change 52,112,137,174
Chaos 59,61,95,144,204,254
Charity 252,256
Charms 148
Chastity 250,256

Chemistry (SEE ALSO ethers) 52,94, 116,123,145,147,151,156,173,174,184, 192,194,203,213,220,223,244,257
Chief virtues 250ff,256
Childhood 157,158,163
China 228,240
Christ 13,24,27,33,49,85,86,97,125, 138,139,140,152,162,182,189,225,228, 250,251
Christian (SEE ALSO church, science) 23ff,33,35,77,83,85,92,95,162,201, 228,250
Church 31,44,110,125,139,250
Cicada 50
Circle 6,68,149,204,210,223,224
Circulation (SEE ALSO blood) 168
Circumcision 96
Cities SEE community AND BY NAME OF EACH
Citizen 108,219
City, sacred 143,136
Civilization 200,224,228,229,235
Clairvoyance (SEE ALSO spiritism) 20, 38,80,96,119,121,122,125,145,157
Classification 165,213,214,233
Climate 74,158
Clymer 31
Cnossus 237
Coccygeal 106
Codex Occultus 43,116,117,172,178ff, 203,220
Cold 123,168
Colonization 96,133,212,228,237,240, 241
Color 88,184,247ff
Communion SEE eucharist, phallic
Community 76,237,238
Comparison 135,170,174,180,203
Competency 120,218
Complexity 93,94,96,100,122,123,126, 151,157,158,182,193,200
Concentration 148,202
Conception 209
Concepts 8,28,39,53,70,170
Concrete thought 131,255
Concurrency 110ff,202,207,249
Confirmation 251,256
Consciousness 26,39,42,43,47,53,54,55, 56,57,65,66,68,75,76,77,80,83,84,85, 89,98,100,102,103,105,114ff,144,146, 148,149,152,153,154,155,156,157,158, 159,161,169,172,184,185,186,187,190, 206,207,209,210,213,214,220,230,239, 241,245,246,248,250,252,256,257
Conservation of mass 52
Consistency 100ff,109,123,126,130,138, 150,151,162,202,207,208,213,221,231, 247
Constantine 24
Consubstantiation 139
Consuming ether 210

Continent 72,76,165,211,212,224,225, 230,231,239,245,257
Contrast 159,247
Cooperation 111,117,124,125,128,140, 149,150,167ff,196,197,198,200,213, 214,215,220,221,231,235,240,243,248
Coordination 62,66,118,149,167,170ff, 184,234,254ff
Copernicus 67
Copt 235
Corpus callosum 173
Correlation 108ff,231
Correspondence 53,110ff,113,115,186, 210,213,233,236,256
Cosmic SEE fire, ocean, universe
Cosmo-Conception, Rosicrucian 70,141, 255
Cosmogony 70,194
Country 75,76
Courage 107
Covetousness 250,256
Crafts 200,238
Creation 61,68,77,81,95,97,103,108, 111,121,167,168,178,184,194,206,253, 254
Creative word 103,108,117
Creed 26,33,187
Crescent, fertile 227
Crete 237
Cretins 162
Critias 73
Cromwell 24
Crops 199
Crookes 127,212,257
Cross (SEE ALSO Calvary) 138,175
Crystallization 82,87,89,95,109,112, 121,135,137,145,162,163,165,166,177, 186,188,190,198,200,201,212,221,232
Cultivation 199,201
Curtiss 31
Cycles 37,44,50,51,52,53,54,55,56,57, 58,65,70,82,90,94,97,99,101,108,133, 135,136,137,140,141,145,155,157,158, 178,185,186,187,193,194,203,205,208, 210,212,214,215,220,225,229,235,236, 237,239,242,253,256
Cyrus 227
Czech 238

Dalton 52
Dane 230
Daniel 64
Darwin 12,215
Day (SEE ALSO creation, epoch) 43,45, 46,47,49,52,98,103,164,205,220,223
Deadly sins 250ff,256
Death 44,96,119,120,122,137,159,188, 195,207
Decad 85,114,115,179,180,237
Decanate (SEE ALSO zodiac) 142
Decay 52,54,65,71,89,102,130,137,198
Deduction 188,190

Degeneration 35,131,134,137,185,200,
224,233,234,247
Deification (SEE ALSO God) 15,189
Delphi 107
Delusion 46,121
Democracy 242
Denial 45,67,83
Dense body SEE mineral, vehicle
Density (SEE ALSO matter) 208
Desire (SEE ALSO astral, emotion, vehicle) 45,104,118,130,136,249
Deutero-Slav 226,238,257
Deviation 99,136,137,140,145,154
Devil 27,42
Diagnosis 54,91
Diana 201,205,206,207,213,257
Diaphragm 107,112,173
Dictionary SEE lexicology
Diet 195
Differentiation (SEE ALSO emanation)
85,127,144,153,157,169,183,201,219,
222,223,226,230,231,234,236,257
Digestion 94
Dimension 39,62,66,69,73,74,77,78,81,
83,94,95,99,115,117,118,120,124,128,
132,134,135,140,145,146,148,149,150,
155,160,164,166,171,175,179,180,181,
183,190,201,208,210,215,219,220,243,
247,254,256
Dimension, fifth 38,117,122,146,254
Dimension, first 78,80,100,104,254
Dimension, fourth 38,78,115,146,254
Dimension, second 78,80,101,102,115,
148,254
Dimension, seventh 146,254
Dimension, sixth 146,254
Dimension, third 78,80,104,115,254
Directions 64,65
Disease 54,113,147
Dissolution (SEE ALSO pralaya) 89,95,
97
Distance 66,70,145,148,164,171
Divergence 126,193,214
Divination 108,133,186,256
Divine SEE science, spirit
Divinity 48,69,108,134,138,139,150,
180,184,200,201,205
Division SEE attenuation, fission, mathematics
Doctrine (SEE ALSO dogma) 28ff
Doctrine, The Secret 70
Dogma 8,188,190
Domain 39,50,51,52,56,57,58,68,70,77,
80,82,84,89,90ff,117,118,119,122,124,
126,127,134,135,137,139,140,145,150,
151,152,153,154,155,162,163,164,183,
184,190,194,196,197,198,201,204,206,
207,208,214,215,217,231,234,240,246,
247
Domestication 110,199,200,201
Dominions 201,254

Double SEE ethers, vehicle
Dot 78,254
Dramatization 173,225,232
Dravidian 226,227,238
Dreams 77,109,121,122,125
Drinkwater 225
Duad 106,109,110,111,112,116,117,
127,128,129,131,134,135,136,138,140,
141,142,144,153,160,162,165,167,168,
169,170,174,175,176,177,178,180,181,
186,190,192,197ff,208,209,215,221,
231
Dual personality 140
Duration SEE time
Dutch 230

Ear 168
Earth 106,251,256
Earth, the 65,67,69,70,71,91,97,98,112,
129,131,138,165,183,204,205,206,207,
208,210,211,212,222,223,232,233,240,
241,242,245,246,247,257
East 39,107,149,179,194,228,242
Eccentricity 82,136
Ecclesia, Mt. 212
Ecliptic SEE obliquity, zodiac
Ecstasy 83,123,136,170,250,252
Eddy 12,60
Eden 112
Egg 68,106
Ego (SEE ALSO absolute, atom, spirits
planetary) 91,97,104,122,132,150,
151,154,155,158,168,169,198,207,
225ff,254
Egypt 56,179,185,225,226,227,236,237
Eight SEE octad
Elementals 92,106,147,244,245,247,
254
Elements SEE air, alchemy, chemistry,
earth, fire, water
Elijah 35
Emanation (SEE ALSO differentiation)
58,80,85,95,101,111,113,114,116,122,
167,170,181,182,185,187,190,201,204,
206,219,221,236,248
Embryology 53,58,157,183,207
Emerson 60
Emigration 224,226ff,236
Emotion (SEE ALSO animal, astral, passion) 88,105,110,118,120,122,130,
154,156
English (SEE ALSO language) 75,166,
226,229,230,231,236
Ennead 114,117,180,237,249,250
Ensoulment 115,151,190
Entities SEE ego, elementals, spiritism
Environment 159,192,193,196,197,201,
214,248
Envy 251,256
Epidemics 90,98
Epigenesis 193,215

Epoch 45,52,70,158,209,211,224,225, 231,239,242,243,246,251,257
Equator 75,211
Equilibrium 74,168
Equinox 40,64,142,165,212
Esdraelon 243
Esoteric 7,14,38,52,56,57,58,83,188, 200
Esoteric Buddhism 255
Essence SEE ethers
Essenes 138
Eternity 45,59,96,110,125,144,182
Etheric plane (SEE ALSO ethers) 123, 128,129,130,201,209,210,255
Etheric state 209,212,213,257
Ethers (SEE ALSO plane, vehicle) 89, 101ff,112,118,121,129,130,131,138, 152,159,163,168,177,206,210,241,243, 244,245
Ethics 20,126
Eucharist 138,139,152,250,256
Eurasia 226,230,234
Europe 74,75,228,242
Evidence 9,120,196
Evil 110,244
Evolution 110,116,122,124,128,133, 141,151,152,153,154,162,169,175,178, 182,183,186,187,188,189,192ff,220, 226,231,233,235,236,238,239,240,241, 243,244,245,246,247,248
Exaltation (SEE ALSO ecstasy) 126,186
Exalting Ether 210
Existence SEE being
Experience 48,68,109,120,122,123,126, 136,162,185,186,187,189,209,213,218, 224,250,253
Expression 114,118,125,128,130,134, 138,140,153,162,167ff,196,215,220, 222
Eye 79,109,168,240
Ezekiel 64,141,228

Facts 160,161,164,165,166,213
Faculty (SEE ALSO senses) 42,70,91, 148,155,157,160,163,249
Fairy 106
Faith 8,48,107,250,256
Family race 179,228,230
Father 85,95,117
Fear 88,107,147,251
Fellowship, Rosicrucian 141,142
Feminine 169,170,175,176,177
Fertile crescent 227
Fertility 71,100
Filipinos 234
Finger prints 187
Finn 226
Fire 133,199,205,251,255,256
Fire plane 129,134,138,246,255
Fission 169
Fittest, survival of 214

Five SEE pentad
Fixity (SEE ALSO crystallization, pattern) 148,177,178
Flagellation 136
Flame 95,106,227
Flesh 139,169,247,250,256
Flood SEE cataclysm
Fluidity 101,103,110,121
Focal SEE center, manifestation, nucleus, position fourth
Food 44,195,199
Force 65,69,80,85,95,172,181,184,194, 205,215,223,245,254,256
Form (SEE ALSO mental, pattern) 47, 52,55,56,61,62,65,66,68,70,81,85,87ff, 104,105,114,116,122,123,127,130,132, 134,135,137,140,144,145,148,150,152, 153,157,161,164,165,166,167,168,170, 172,174,175,177,178,184,186,192,193, 196,197,198,202,206,212,216,220,221, 231,232,254
Fortitude 251,256
Fortune-tellers (SEE ALSO prophecy, spiritism) 21,49,76
Four SEE tetrad
Fourfold 105,159,169,206
Fourth SEE dimension, gospel, human, position, state
Fourth estate 127,212
French 73,75,76,229,230,231
Freud 136
Function 54,91,95,109,112,128,134, 151,153,157,168,173,174,185,186,192, 196,198

Garlic 148
Galilee 243
Garment, solar wedding 104
Gaseous 127,203,209,212,213,257
Gastric juices 195
Gemini 12
Generation 192,193,197
Genesis 194,224,247
Genghis Khan 228
Genoese 231
Geocentric 67
Geography 72,227,243
Geology 58,73,99,187,205,208,211
Geometry 65,72,84,145,150,179,184, 214,236,241,256
German SEE Swiss, Teufonic
Ghost SEE Holy Spirit, spiritism
Gift 106,107
Gipsies 227
Glands 102,106,110,173,195,196,212
Globe (SEE ALSO earth the, sphere) 70,209
Gluttony 250,256
Gnomes 244
Gobi 224,236
God 17,25,43,48,69,84,99,144,150,169, 179,194,217

Goiter 195
Gold 236,248,257
Golden SEE age, aura, brotherhoods, truth
Golden Gates, City of the 224
Gomorrah 238
Goshen 224
Gospel, Fourth 86,225
Grace 194
Grains 199
Gravitation 34,65,95,172
Great Central Flame 95,227
Greek 226,229,230,231,234,237
Green 248,257
Gregorian 40
Growth 52,54,65,101,104,107,112,116, 123,125,130,136,157,158,183,193,195, 201,202,211,218,219,248,251,254
Guilds 200

Habit 82,130,136,138,166
Harmony 48,170,172,184
Healing 119,142,250
Hearing 148
Heart 51,107,173
Heat 103,168,241
Heaven 20,36,44,55,63,77,92,119,130, 205
Heavenly bodies 103,129,131,148,165
Hebrew SEE Jew
Heindel 12,31,70,141,142,208,255
Heliocentric 67
Hell 44,119,130,251
Hemisphere (SEE ALSO cerebral) 74,234
Hepatogenic 212,246,257
Heptad 114,127,129,142,158,180,181, 201,204,208,210,219ff,256,257
Heredity 55,193
Hermaphrodite 169
Hermes 32,63,84
Hexad 204,210,215,220,221,230,236, 237
Hexagram 203
Hibernation 50
Hierarchies (SEE ALSO brotherhoods, initiates, initiation) 124,133,134,200, 201,254
Hieratic 179,225,228,247
Hindu 226,227
History 58,83,224,225,226,229,233, 234,235,237
Hittite 234,235
Holy SEE palestine, week
Holy Rollers 31
Holy Spirit 95,117
Homeopathy 113
Homes of Truth 31
Hope 251,256
Horoscopy (SEE ALSO astrology, fortune-tellers) 12,53,64,75,76,77,115,173, 175,176

Horoscope, The Progressed 50
Horse 199,235
Hour 45,220,223
Human (SEE ALSO body, man, soul, spirit) 35,53,54,70,80,88,91,93,94, 98,105,112,116,118,122,128,131,136, 137,138,150,154,158,159,162,163,169, 193,198,200,201,206,207,209,211,212, 213,217,224ff,254
Humanitarian 124,132
Hungarian 226,228,229,242,244
Hyperborean 211,226,239,245,257
Hypotheses (SEE ALSO concepts) 18, 28,53,160,189,214,219
Hypnosis 30,51,102

Identity 125,145,172
Idiosyncrasy 82,136
Idiot 163,239
Illuminati 252
Illumination SEE initiation
Illusion 37ff,67,70,84,85,125,135,145, 148,164,188
Imagination (SEE ALSO reflection) 20, 36,55,68,77,79,81,104,119,121,122, 125,130,131,159,164,177,189,221
Immigration 224,226ff,236
Impulse SEE activity, emanation, force, reflex
Incarnation 122,151,182,206,232,239, 249,253
Indestructibility 33,52,65,71,95,96,194
India 226,227,228,238
Indian, American 74,123,233,235,236, 238,239
Individuality 48,54,87,89,155,169,237, 253
Individualization 99,144,175,177,186, 247
Indo-Iranic 226,227,257
Induction 103,159,187ff,193,195
Inertia 100,104,116,254
Infancy 158,159,207,209
Infinity 62,146,147,148,149,171
Initiate (SEE ALSO brotherhoods, hierarchies) 49,99,124,132,133,188,210, 241,242,245,249,252,253
Initiation 13,19,23,33,35,56,57,96,104, 106,107,117,125,126,128,133,138,139, 141,149,163,182,183,185,200,201,205, 212,215,217,218,237,244,246,248ff, 256
Insanity 22,128,156
Instinct SEE consciousness, mind
Instruction 7,9,13,38,56,96,117,119, 161,163,188,189,210,219,225,232,234, 244,247,251
Intellectualism 10,126,194
Intelligence (SEE ALSO ego, memory) 80,103,126,144,154,155,156,158,161, 163,188,189,195,205,240,244,247

Interbreeding 233,235
Interchange 47,48,53,65,68,69,71,75,
76,164,185,211,232,240,243
Internationalism 72
Interoceanic 233,234
Interpretation 108,217
Intestines 94,195
Intuition 19,77,133,156,161
Invention 55,66
Inversion (SEE ALSO perversion) 96,
126,128,153,167,198,209,237
Involution 124,178,197,198,200,202,
206,212,220,247
Iranic 226,227,257
Iridiagnosis 32
Irish 236
Iron 223,235
Irregularity 51,136,137
Islam 228
Italic 205,226,229,230,231,235,237,257

Janus 201,205,206,207,213,257
Japanese 228,229,240
Jehovah 72,134,179
Jeremiah 96
Jerusalem 142,227,243
Jesus (SEE ALSO Christ) 139
Jew 27,35,74,96,203,226,228,235
John the Baptist 35
John the Divine 13,85,86,106,107,225
Jonah 72
Jones 31
Judge 208,255
Julian 40
Jupiter 142,205,206,207,213,223,254,
256,257

Kabala 27,106,113,228
Kaiser 76
Kant 12,252
Karma 34,106,132,134,183,188,251
Key SEE truths
Key to Theosophy, The 255
Keys to knowledge 58,110,181ff,190,256
Khan, Genghis 228
Kingdom (SEE ALSO animal, domain,
human, mineral, vegetable) 92ff,151,
153,164,254
Kingdom of Heaven 77,84
Knowledge (SEE ALSO keys) 8,20,39,
57,58,67,109,156,160,161,162,164,
165,171,183,185,186,187,188,189,213,
216,217,219,251,252
Korea 228
Krotona 212

Laggards 75,88,201,232,235,236,238,
239,243
Language 16,73,217,230
Latin 73,205
Lavoisier 52

Law, chemical 52,71
Law, natural 11,30,35,54,56,65,68,87,
92,116,119,178,180,188,194,197,201,
215,249
Laws SEE Codex Occultus, keys to
knowledge
Lead 223
Leadbeater 208
Left (SEE ALSO black) 253
Lemurian 73,89,211,226,232,233,237,
243,244,245,247,257
Leo 50,173
Leprosy 148
Letts 236,238
Lewis 31
Lexicology 16,32,101,119,127,197,205,
208,211,212,232,233,237,249
Liberal Catholic Church 31
Libido 170
Libra 12,173
Life (SEE ALSO ethers, spirit, stream)
48,50,93,94,96,128,130,134,151,173,
186,193,196,202,216,219,250
Light (SEE ALSO astral, ethers, years)
103
Limitation 39,91,93,103,109,145,212,
240,254
Lincoln 225
Line 78,254
Liquid 127,203,209,212,213,257
Lithuanian 236,238
Liver 212
Locusts 50
Lodge SEE brotherhoods, white
Logos 201,254
Loyola 24
Loma, Point 212
Lords 201,240
Lotus 54
Love SEE passion
Lunar (SEE ALSO schools) 96
Lunar ocean 113,132,223
Lunar plane 128,130,131,147,163,168,
209,245,255
Lust 250,256
Luther 24
Lycanthrophy 162
Lymphatic system 169

Macrocosm 33,69,97,113,152,183
Magic SEE spiritism
Magyar 226,228,229,242,244
Mahatma (SEE ALSO initiation) 15
Malay 234
Male SEE masculine
Man (SEE ALSO human, races) 17,73,
94,97,99,102,103,104,105,108,110,
113,118,123,131,132,133,134,152,157,
162,169,178,179,183,188,193,194,199,
201,206,210,211,215,218,219,224ff,
255,257
Manchus 226,228,240

Manichean 227,244,245,248
Manifestation 103,111,127,129,150,
  154,162,192,203,217ff,254
Mantra 148
Manvantara 46,103
Marriage 250,256
Marriage of the philosophers 247
Mars 205,223,228,240,241,242,244,
  254,256,257
Masculine 169,170,175,176,177
Masonic SEE Rosicrucian
Mass (SEE ALSO eucharist, matter) 61,
  75,116,134,148,150,151,182,184,200,
  232
Mass, conservation of 52
Masses 44,55,161
Master SEE initiation
Masturbation 136
Mathematics 40,63,65,78,115,117,128,
  173,215,237
Matrimony 250,256
Matrix 135,221,225
Matter (SEE ALSO state) 65,69,71,74,
  80,95,103,112,114,118,127,129,131,
  135,140,146,150,153,177,184,186,194,
  206,209,210,212,232,243,244,250,257
Matthew 95
Maturity 158,159
Mayas 179,236
Mazdaznan 31
Measure SEE dimension, distance, size,
  time
Medicine 89,113,147,162,194,195,217
Mediterranean 148,229
Memory (SEE ALSO *akasa,* tradition)
  56,104,161
Memphite 179,226
Mendeleeff 52
Mendelism 193
Menstruation 21,47,50
Mental 77,84,118,120,121,130,131,
  147,154,155,156,159,161,177,229
Mental plane 129,132,155,255
Mental world 128,132,133,134,138,
  155,255
Mercury 205,222,223,241,254,256,257
Mesopotamia 227
Metabolism 72,138,168,199,213,257
Metals (SEE ALSO BY NAME OF EACH)
  223
Metaphor 173,174
Metaphysics SEE philosophy
Metempsychosis 35
Meteor 71,131
Mexican 233,247
Microcosm 32,69,97,105,112,113,147,
  152,182,183
Migration 99,232,235
Mind (SEE ALSO mental) 154ff,187,
  201,209,255
Minoan 226

Mineral 54,80,92,93,94,97,98,100,101,
  103,109,112,116,123,125,150,151,156,
  158,159,162,163,198,199,201,241,246,
  254
Miracles (SEE ALSO spiritism) 30,34,
  90
Miscegenation 233,240
Mithraic 227
Mohammed 26,228
Monad 84,85,86,111,115,116,117,140,
  166,169,179,180,190,208,215,222,236,
  237
Mongolian 226,228,238,239,240,242,
  244
Monotheism 48
Month 45,47,49,164
Mood 90,121,188,194
Moon 40,183,205,222,223,232,254,
  256,257
Mormonism 31
Moron 155,163
Moses 224,225
Mother 95
Motion, lords of 201
Motions (SEE ALSO force, movement)
  52,53,65,67,80,115,184
Mount Ecclesia 212
Mouth 168
Movement (SEE ALSO motions) 104,
  116,137,168
Movements SEE schools, sociology
Mulatto 233
Multiple proportions 52
Mummification 33
Muscular-nervous system 169
Music 168,184
Meyer 52
Mysteries 52,57,83,96,107,138,141,
  142,161,181,185,187,188,189,221,224,
  227,228,246,247,249
Myths (SEE ALSO tradition) 97,182

Name (SEE ALSO lexicology) 218
National 75,76,200,229,230
Natural SEE law, selection
Nature (SEE ALSO *akasa,* brotherhoods,
  elementals, function, Rosicrucian, sub-
  stance, vehicle) 17,157,166,192,194,
  195,197,206,215,216,217,220,245
Navel 107
Near East 179
Negative (SEE ALSO feminine) 96,136,
  174,202
Negro 74,232
Neo-Platonic 147
Neptune 193,222,254
Nerves 110,168,169,173
Neurotic 10,148
Newcomb 40
Newlands 52
New Thought 31,60

Newton 34,65
New Zealand 226
Night (SEE ALSO *pralaya*) 50,103
Nine SEE ennead
Nirvana 26,39
Noah 232
Normality 51,136,147,154,162,195,215
North 242
North America 74,212
Nose 109,145,168,169
Nubian 179
Nucleus 67,77,151,157,206,238
Numerology (SEE ALSO Pythagorean
   AND BY EACH NUMBER) 32,83,108,
   114,115,118,127,128,129,162,164,179,
   180,181,190,203,220,237

Oath 20,200,248
Objective 54,69,70,77,81,92,111,127,
   135,140,176,180,184,185,202,206,256
Obliquity of ecliptic 52,74,99,230
Obsession 35,131,148
Occultus, Codex 43,116,117,172,
   178ff,203,220
Ocean 113,132,133,165,207,223,234
Ocean of Theosophy, The 255
Oceanside 142
Octad 114,117,128,161,162,178,180,
   204,237,252,254,255
Odor 88,168
Oil 250,256
Olive 248,257
One SEE monad
Optic 173
Oracles 245
Orange 248,257
Orbits 52,64,222
Order SEE Chaldean, kingdom, species
Orders SEE Christian, hierarchies, sub-
   empyrean
Ordination 251,256
Organs 110,165,195,196
Origin of species 216
Orthodoxy 26,28,33,95,117,125,138
Oudad 59,60,85,116,117,180
Outline of Occult Science 255
Ovaries 195
Overlapping 99,137,211,230,236
Ozone 102

Palate 195
Pallid 248,257
Palestine 140,226,227,235,243
Palmistry   SEE fortune-tellers, signatures
Pandean 88,89,99,245,246
Pantheistic 48,215
Paracelsus 13,113
Paraclete 95,117
Parathyroid 195
Passion 88,107,123,163

Pattern (SEE ALSO form) 39,65,81,82,
   89,95,96,97,99,104,105,108,133,145,
   150,157,164,165,177,183,193,195,198,
   214,221,238
Paul 24
Penance 248,251,256
Pentad 114,125,168,169,176,177,181,
   190,215,221,236,237,242
Perception SEE mind, understanding
Perennials 50,56
Perfume 88,123
Periodic system 52
Periods 70,98,201,204ff,213,225,246,
   257
Persian (SEE ALSO Indo-Iranic) 27,92
Persistence 65,82,194
Personality 12,15,126,132,140
Perspective 37,39,41,44,50,51,56,57,58,
   62,70,76,77,81,112,116,125,126,127,
   135,144ff,160,161,163,164,165,177,
   181,209,214,241,251
Perversion 20,128,136,225
Phallic 21,83,106,158,169ff,170,186,
   195,200,222,252,253
Pharyngeal 107
Phenician 226,237
Phenomena SEE activity, spiritism
Philosopher SEE initiate, marriage,
   stone
Philosophy 7,8,25,27,30,78,119,160
Photograph 42,156
Physical SEE matter, mineral
Physical plane 101,123,128,129,200,
   209,246,255
Physical world 122,125,127,128,129,
   130,131,201,210,223,240,255
Phrenology SEE fortune-tellers, signa-
   tures
Pi 149,150
Picture SEE imagination, symbolism
Pineal 96,173,195
Pioneers (SEE ALSO initiate) 201,227
Pisces 12,212
Pituitary 195
Placenta 232
Placidus 65
Plagues 225
Plane (SEE ALSO world) 70,78,119ff,
   138,145,147,155,163,164,168,200,201,
   208,209,210,220,223,241,245,246,254,
   255
Planet (SEE ALSO earth, the) 103,131,
   132,193,223,254
Planets (SEE ALSO astrology, heavenly
   bodies, horoscopy, spirits planetary,
   AND BY NAME OF EACH) 104,115,
   133,142,173,204,205,213,220,222,240,
   241
Plant SEE vegetable
Plantain 99
Plato 73

Plexus, solar 107
Plummer 31
Poetry 119
Point 78,254
Point Loma 212
Point of view SEE perspective
Poise 169
Polarian 211,225,245,246,257
Poles (SEE ALSO duad) 211,238
Polynesian 234,235
Portuguese 230,231
Poseidonian 73,234,235,238
Position, fourth 94,129,203,204,207,
    209,210,221,222,242,246
Positive (SEE ALSO masculine) 96,174,
    202
Postures 107
Power 140,177,215,242
Powers 201,254
Pralaya 103,185,204,219,232
Prana 102,169,255
Precipitate 169,213,257
Precocity 128,162,188
Prediction (SEE ALSO fortune-tellers)
    49,242
Preformation 193
Prejudices 7,130,155
Prescience 77,132,133,156
Pride 252,256
Priest SEE hieratic and sacrament
Principalities 201,254
Principle SEE vehicle
Process (SEE ALSO activity) 69,114,
    134ff,140,145,166,174,175,179,183,
    184,186,187,188,192,196,197,202,203,
    220,222,256,257
Progressed Horoscope, The 50
Projection 79,104
Prophecy (SEE ALSO fortune-tellers,
    spiritism) 107,242,243,253
Prophets 12,60,86,113,141,166,190,215,
    252
Proportions, multiple 52
Prudence 251,256
Psychic SEE astral, fortune-tellers, spir-
    itism
Psycho-analysis 30,90,109,170
Pudding-bags 94,245
Purgatory 130
Purple 248,257
Pyramid 6,167,204,236
Pythagorean 56,58,84,112,114,117,128,
    140,162,165,176,179,180,181,182,190,
    203,215,237,250,254
Pythoness 107

Quadrature (SEE ALSO horoscopy, tetrad)
    149
Quantitative analysis 52
Quetzalcoatl 247
Quimby 60

Races 70,74,75,82,96,124,133,178,179,
    200,211,212,214,224ff,254,257
Rapt 213,257
Rays, emanative 58,114,117,220,221
Reaction (SEE ALSO reflex) 136,140,156
Reality 38,39,46,59,67,114,121,122,
    124,125,126,145,146,149,159,163,164,
    170,184,185,209
Realm SEE domain, plane, sphere,
    world
Rebirth 35,56,132,206
Recapitulation 52,54,55,89,99,101,117,
    155,157,158,166,186,201,208,209,211,
    226,236,242,243,246,249,254,257
Red (SEE ALSO eye, Indian) 233,248,
    257
Reduplication 55,56,104,155
Reflecting ether 104
Reflection 110,112,183,203
Reflex 104,107,116,136,154,155,156,
    159,168,182,192,198
Region SEE plane
Reincarnation 35,56,132,206
Relationship 37,49,52,57,61,62,65,66,
    68,69,75,77,83,84,103,109,112,113,
    140,144,149,150,160,162,164,166,170,
    171,172,173,174,175,182,183,184,185,
    197,202,203,210,214,217,219,221,230,
    231,252,256
Religion 8,25,27,83,123,194,197,227,
    250
Repercussion 90,156
Repetition (SEE ALSO recapitulation)
    51,56,101
Repression 84,136
Resolution (SEE ALSO attenuation) 65,
    113,129,172,185
Resonance 169
Resolvent 213,257
Resurrection 33
Retardation 137
Revelation (SEE ALSO apocalypse, spirit-
    ism, tradition) 8,13,20,78,168,189
Reversal (SEE ALSO perspective) 250
Reversion 199
Revolution (SEE ALSO earth the, round)
    52
Rmoahal 232,233,234
Right SEE angle, white
Rigor mortis 54,100,102,137
Rip Van Winkle 41
Rites 30,83,96,138,170,187,200,247,
    250,252
Roman 73,205,229,231,237
Romance 73,205
Romany 227
Root SEE cassava, crops, stuff
Root races 211,212,224ff,257
Rosicrucian (SEE ALSO Fellowship, Soci-
    etas) 31,59,92,102,106,118,119,127,
    129,141,185,201,204,205,208,209,213,
    228,237,242,244,245,247,248,255,257

Rosicrucian Cosmo-Conception 70,
141,204,205,208,209,255
Roumanian 230
Round 98,208,209,241
Russell 31
Russia 238,242

Sabbath 47,104
Sabian 179,235,236,237,238
Sabine 205
Sacral 106
Sacrament 30,138,247,248ff,256
Sacrifice 106,117,138,182,247
Sagittarius 12
Salamanders 244
Salvation SEE atonement
Samana 169
Samuel 96
Satan 27,42
Satiation 45,105,136
Saturn 142,201,205,206,207,210,213,
222,223,246,254,256,257
Scandinavia 224,230
Schools (SEE ALSO instruction, myster-
ies) 9,11,28,30,58,84,111,112,118,
119,128,140,146,154,165,177,190,200,
203,215,218,219,244,248,252
Science, Christian 31,60
Science, Divine 31
Science, material 8,11,24,27,38,53,55,
57,58,65,67,69,73,74,90,92,93,120,
127,145,147,160,162,163,166,173,182,
189,190,192,193,194,195,197,212,213,
214,225,228,234,237,252
Science, Outline of Occult 255
Scofield 31
Scythian 234
Sea (SEE ALSO ocean) 107
Seal, Solomon's 140,203
Season (SEE ALSO cycles) 50
Secret Doctrine, The 70
Seed 97,104,123,193,205
Seed-atom 107,132,150,152,153,159,
169,193,207
Selection, natural 213ff
Self SEE consciousness, ego
Semicircular canals 168
Semitic 225,226,227,234,235,237,257
Sensation 121,168,186
Senses (SEE ALSO mind AND BY NAME
OF EACH) 17,43,49,148,156,168,221
Separation 61,89,104,111,116,128,132,
145,150,169,177,183,187,200,202
Serpent 106
Seven SEE heptad
Sex SEE phallic, poles
Sextile 12
Sheath SEE vehicle
Shells 121,122,130,160
Sidon 237
Sight 79,148,156,169

Signs SEE zodiac
Signatures 164ff,167,173,179,214,216,
233,240
Simile 173,174
Sin-born 233
Sinnett 208,241,255
Sins, deadly 250ff,256
Sinus 145,169
Situation 67,69,165,183
Six SEE hexad
Sixteen 129,237
Size 70,148,171
Skill 109,218
Skin 109,169
Sky 107
Slavonic 226,230,238,257
Sleep 44,50,51,77,98,208
Sloth 251,256
Smell SEE nose
Sociology 126,159,187,202,218
Socializing ether 210
Societas Rosicruciana in America 36
Socrates 188
Sodom 238
Solar (SEE ALSO breaths, consciousness,
mysteries, myth) 96
Solar plane 129,132,133,138,255
Solar plexus 107
Solar system 98,99,133,222,254
Solar wedding garment 104
Solid (SEE ALSO matter) 78,101,127,
145,166,203,209,212,254,257
Solmon's seal 140,203
Solstice 64,142
Solvent 213,257
Somatic SEE centers
Son (SEE ALSO Christ) 95,97,117
Soul 139,141,155,169,255
South America 74,212,235
Space (SEE ALSO state) 44,61ff,77,87,
95,96,101,103,108,111,114,140,144,
146,148,153,161,164,180,182,186,190,
207,209,210,213,254,257
Spanish 229,230,231,238
Spark SEE absolute, ego
Specialization 73,93,103,109,111,123,
125,126,134,136,140,151,152,153,161,
176,177,178,180,182,186,187,192,196,
197,198,199,200,201,202,206,212,217,
218,219,232,238,241
Species 82,132,139,173,177,193,198,
199,201,213ff
Spectrum 213,220,223,224
Sphere (SEE ALSO domain) 63,66,71,
76,82,84,92,108,117,125,126,127,129,
132,137,145,150,164,166,182,183,194,
196,215,232,254
Spine 106,112,173
Spirit 95,117,153,155,177,185,201,202,
232,247,255
Spirit plane 134,255
Spirit world 128,133,207,255

Spiritism (SEE ALSO fortune-tellers, pro-
phecy) 18,19,30,34,77,83,91,99,108,
109,119,121,125,130,131,145,147,159,
160,162,225,243,245,249,253
Spirits SEE absolute, atom, ego, ele-
mentals, spirit
Spirits, planetary 133,152,201,223,246,
250,254
Spirituous 213,257
Spring 107,123,205
Square 6,204
Star SEE geometry, heavenly bodies,
planets, worship, zodiac
State (SEE ALSO consciousness, matter,
space) 116,127,129,130,202,203,204,
205,207,208,209,210,212,213,220,248,
256
State, fourth 127,212
Steiner 31,208,255
Stimulation 83,89,90,118,136,139,236
Stone, philosopher's 82
Stragglers, SEE laggards
Stratification 136,137,140
Stream, life 91,94,98,164,169,170,198,
200,201,210,225,232,233,239,241,243,
245,246,254
Stuff, root 61,82,219
Stupidity 154,162
Subconscious (SEE ALSO mental, subjec-
tive) 90,119,130
Subempyrean 92,201,210
Subjective 54,69,70,77,81,92,111,127,
135,140,176,180,197,202,206
Sublimate (SEE ALSO ethers) 213,257
Subraces 224ff,257
Substance (SEE ALSO matter, stuff root)
44,46,52,56,59,61,65,68,70,71,85,87,
93,94,95,96,97,104,105,108,109,111,
114ff,144,146,150,151,156,166,167,
168,170,174,175,176,184,185,190,198,
203,206,212,213,243
Succession SEE cycles, state
Successor 251
Sufi 26
Suicide 122
Sumerian 226,236
Sun 40,67,123,133,142,173,205,222,
241,254,256,257
Superstition 162,189
Suppression 84,136
Suprarenal 195
Surgery 82,195,217
Survival of fittest 214
Swedenborg 31
Swiss 230,231
Sylphs 244
Symbolism 16,17,64,83,103,108,135,
138,161,162,164,169,173,178,180,189,
200,205,206,218,220,223,225,243,249
Synthesis 197,215,219
Syria 227,235

Tables, planetary 142
Tapioca 199
Tartar 226
Tasmanian 233
Taste 168,169
Tau 176
Taurus 12
Teacher SEE initiate, instruction,
schools
Tellus 205,207,213,225,257
Temperance 251,256
Temperature 98,101,203
Temple 125,141,142,185,189,203,236,
247,252
Ten SEE decad
Tendency 55,82,89,130,132,137,138,
178,197ff,199,214
Testes 195
Tests 120
Tetrad 116,117,119,127,128,165,166,
167,179,180,190,204,210,215,220,221,
237,242,249
Tetragrammaton 179
Teutonic 76,226,229,230,231,235,236,
257
Text-books 12,50,197,208
Theosophical Society 238
Theosophy 7,31,35,59,85,94,118,119,
166,169,204,205,208,209,213,241,255,
257
Theosophy, The Key to 255
Theosophy, The Ocean of 255
Thought SEE form, mental, mind, New,
volition
Thought, concrete 131,255
Thread 197,207
Three SEE triad
Throat 107
Thrones 201,254
Time 37ff,62,65,70,79,84,85,87,95,96,
103,108,111,114,121,140,144,145,153,
161,164,174,175,177,178,180,210,211,
215,254
Timaeus 73
Tissue (SEE ALSO flesh) 110,173,195,
196
Tlavatli 232,233,234
Tolerance 107,124,251
Toltec 233,234,235,238
Tolstoy 242
Tone 169,184
Tongue (SEE ALSO language) 108,168
Touch 168,169
Tradition 9,38,99,106,127,133,160,
166,169,183,188,192,200,204,212,218,
224,225,227,230,232,244,245,247,249
Transcendence 59,79,132
Transcendentalism 31,60,214
Transmigration 35
Transmutation 33,65,184,213,244
Transubstantiation 138,139

Triad 114,116,117,119,128,129,140,
165,166,167,168,175,176,177,179,180,
190,203,204,208,210,212,215,220,221,
225,231,237,243,249
Triangle 6,140,167,177,203,204
Trigonometry 135
Trinity 95,111,114,117
Troy 226,237
Truth 10,174,188,219,225,252
Truth, golden 1,48,61,87,95,108,149,
165,170,184,217
Truth, homes of 31
Truths, key 9,28,37,44,48,58,61,87,
114,117,119,144,153,167,180,192,196,
201,217,219,220
Turanian 234
Turk 226,228,229,234
Two SEE duad
Twelve 125,204
Type (SEE ALSO races, shells, species)
130,177,193,198,199,231,233,240

Udana 169
Umbilicus 107
Unction 250,256
Understanding (SEE ALSO mind) 7,37,
39,46,51,57,59,62,67,107,108,111,112,
114,127,155,158,161,162,164,168,172,
179,180,183,187ff,190,196,197,198,
203,204,207,210,213,216,219,250,251
Undines 244
Unit 48,76,248
United States (SEE ALSO Yankee) 73,
75,76,236
Unity 31,59,61,69,72,76,84,85,87,111,
124,129,145,150,222
Universalization 110,111,136,140,153,
176,178,192,197,198,201,202,206,213,
232
Universe 69,95,97,145,146,173,183,
192,212,215,221,222,252,254,255
Ural-Altaic 141,226,228,237,239,240,
242,244,257
Uranus 12,193,222,254
Urge (SEE ALSO emanation, force) 114,
169
Urogenital 168

Valence 52,220
Vanity 59,126
Vapor, spinal 106
Vascular-pulmonary system 169
Vedanta 31
Vegetable 54,71,72,74,80,88,92,93,94,
98,100,101,102,103,110,112,116,118,
123,132,150,151,158,159,162,163,198,
199,201,207,241,245,254

Vehicle 65,69,70,92,118,125,129 133,
134,137,150ff,155,157,158,159,161,
162,163,164,168,169,177,188,206,207,
240,244,255
Veil 39,119,130,251
Venetian 231
Venus 88,99,133,205,206,207,213,223,
240,241,242,245,246,254,256,257
Vermiform appendix 88,212
Versatility 200,218
Vibration (SEE ALSO activity) 101,102,
105,112,156,167,176,184
Vicarious atonement 26,85,117,138,
139,182,194
Virtues 201,250ff,254,256
Vitality (SEE ALSO vehicle) 107,255
Vitamins 195
Voice 107,168
Volition 130,169,173
Voodooism 245
Vulcan 205,206,207,210,213,257

Warp thread 197,207
Wasps 99
Water 251,256
Weather 74,98,103,123
Wedding garment 104
Week 45,47,164
Welsh 236
Wesley 24
White (SEE ALSO brotherhoods, spirit-
ism) 247,248,257
White Lodge 124,126,246,248,252
Will SEE volition
Winter 50,123
Wisdom 8,36,58,188,205,217,251
Wisdom, The Ancient 255
Woman SEE feminine
Wombat 88,89
Word (SEE ALSO lexicology) 103,108,
117
World 70,119ff,134,138,155,164,194,
201,206,207,208,210,220,223,231,240,
255
Worship, star 179,235

Yankee 226,229,230,231,235,236,237,
238,242,257
Year 43,45,47,49,50,52,164
Years, light 66,148
Yellow 240,248,257
Youth 158,159
Yucatan 179,236
Yvana 169

Zero SEE oudad
Zodiac 64,96,115,142,165,173,179,183,
184,212,256
Zoroaster 27